MAYER SMITH

The Crying Wolf and the Darkest Night

Copyright © 2025 by Mayer Smith

All rights reserved. No part of this publication may be reproduced, stored or transmitted in any form or by any means, electronic, mechanical, photocopying, recording, scanning, or otherwise without written permission from the publisher. It is illegal to copy this book, post it to a website, or distribute it by any other means without permission.

This novel is entirely a work of fiction. The names, characters and incidents portrayed in it are the work of the author's imagination. Any resemblance to actual persons, living or dead, events or localities is entirely coincidental.

Mayer Smith asserts the moral right to be identified as the author of this work.

Mayer Smith has no responsibility for the persistence or accuracy of URLs for external or third-party Internet Websites referred to in this publication and does not guarantee that any content on such Websites is, or will remain, accurate or appropriate.

Designations used by companies to distinguish their products are often claimed as trademarks. All brand names and product names used in this book and on its cover are trade names, service marks, trademarks and registered trademarks of their respective owners. The publishers and the book are not associated with any product or vendor mentioned in this book. None of the companies referenced within the book have endorsed the book.

First edition

This book was professionally typeset on Reedsy. Find out more at reedsy.com

Contents

1	The Howl in the Dark	1
2	The Stranger's Touch	8
3	The Secret of the Howl	15
4	Whispers in the Wind	22
5	The Full Moon's Grip	29
6	The Curse Unveiled	35
7	The Midnight Duel	42
8	A Night of Shadows	49
9	The Rising Darkness	56
10	Betrayal in the Moonlight	63
11	The Broken Sea	70
12	A Forbidden Kiss	77
13	The Hunt Begins	83
14	The Heart of the Wolf	90
15	The Rising Moon	97
16	The Breaking Point	104
17	The Love That Binds	111
18	The Ancient War	117
19	The Darkest Night	123
20	The Fall of the Beast	129
21	A Heart's Sacrifice	136
22	The Moon's Last Gaze	143
23	The Return of the Shadows	150
24	The Reckoning	156

25 The Dawn of a New Moon 163

One

The Howl in the Dark

Scene 1: The Crying Wolf

The town of Ashgrove lies in a deep, shadowy valley. Ancient trees, twisted by centuries of wind and rain, stand like silent sentinels over the sleepy streets. The moon, full and pale, hangs heavy in the sky, casting an eerie glow upon the town's forgotten corners. The wind howls through the forest, stirring the leaves like whispers of long-buried secrets.

Kieran stands at the edge of the forest, his figure silhouetted against the rising moon. His eyes are closed, his breath shallow, as if every exhale takes more from him than the last. He knows what is coming. The curse. The agony. The howl.

Kieran's muscles tense. His jaw tightens as he fights to keep the change at bay. But it is futile. The moon calls to him. It beckons like a siren, drawing him closer to the inevitable. His body begins to tremble, and his hands clench into fists as fur sprouts from his skin. His bones contort, his senses blur with the oncoming frenzy.

Kieran howls, a sound filled with sorrow and rage, an echo that shakes the very earth beneath him.

Kieran: (Voice raw, desperate) No... Not tonight... Not again.

The howl rips through the night like a cry of a dying animal, heart-wrenching, filled with a loneliness that could tear apart the heavens. The wind carries the sound across the valley, into the town of Ashgrove, where every resident knows the meaning of the cry. They've heard it before. And they know it will come again.

Scene 2: Elara's Arrival

Elara stands on the outskirts of Ashgrove, her silhouette bathed in the moonlight. She's just arrived, drawn to the town by something she cannot explain, a pull that seems to come from deep within her. She holds her coat tightly around her, feeling an unfamiliar chill in the air. Her heart pounds in her chest, the rhythm erratic, as if it's attuned to something more than the night.

The howl reaches her ears. It's a sound unlike any she's ever heard—a guttural, mournful cry that tugs at something inside her. Her breath catches in her throat, and for a moment, she stands frozen, her eyes wide. There is something so primal

The Howl in the Dark

about the howl, so full of pain and longing, that it feels as if the cry is meant for her alone.

Elara: (Softly, to herself) What... was that?

She takes a hesitant step forward, her boots crunching on the dirt path. Something about the sound pulls her closer, the way the ocean pulls at a ship caught in its tide. She doesn't understand why, but she feels as though she's been called. The air is thick with an otherworldly tension, as if the very land itself is holding its breath.

The wind picks up, swirling around her, and for a moment, she's sure she hears whispers—voices in the wind, faint and fragmented. Her fingers tremble as she clutches her coat tighter around her shoulders. She has always been drawn to the unknown, to the things that others fear or cannot see. And tonight, it feels as though the unknown is waiting for her, beckoning her into the heart of the mystery.

Scene 3: The Search for the Source

Elara makes her way through the narrow, winding streets of Ashgrove, her footsteps quick but hesitant. She's not sure why she's drawn here—why she feels compelled to search for the source of the howl. But as she walks, she senses that something is watching her, waiting for her. It's as if the very night is alive, aware of her presence.

The town is silent, unnervingly so. The houses are dark, their windows shuttered against the night. Only the occasional flicker of candlelight from behind closed curtains offers any sign of life. The streets are empty, save for the shadows that stretch long and thin in the moonlight.

She passes an old, crumbling church at the edge of town, its bell tower towering over her. The church is abandoned, the doors long since rotted away, but something about it calls to her. She pauses, her breath coming in quick gasps as the howl reaches her again. It's closer now, louder, more desperate.

Elara: (To herself, determined) I need to find it. I need to know what it is.

Her pulse quickens as she turns down a narrow alleyway, the darkness enveloping her. The howl echoes again, this time so close that she can feel the vibration in her bones. It sends a shiver of both fear and fascination through her. She walks faster now, her feet carrying her without thinking, drawn inexorably toward the sound.

Scene 4: The Encounter

The alley opens up into a clearing at the edge of the forest. Elara stops, her eyes widening as she sees him. Kieran stands in the center of the clearing, his form towering and monstrous, his body half-human, half-beast. His hair is wild, his eyes glowing with an eerie light. His chest heaves with each breath, and his claws dig into the earth as though he's trying to hold onto his humanity, but it's slipping away from him.

Kieran: (His voice a tortured growl) Leave… before it's too late.

The Howl in the Dark

Elara stands frozen, her heart hammering in her chest. She knows, in that moment, that this is the source of the howl—the man, or rather the creature, that has haunted her thoughts since she first heard the cry. Her eyes lock with his, and she feels a strange pull, a magnetic force that binds her to him. It's as if they've known each other forever, though they've never met.

Elara: (Voice soft, trembling) You... You're the one... The one who howls.

Kieran looks at her, his gaze conflicted. There's pain in his eyes, and something darker—something primal, dangerous. He's fighting it, fighting the curse that tears at him, pulling him between man and beast.

Kieran: (Desperate) I warned you. Go. You shouldn't be here. It's too dangerous.

Elara takes a step forward, her instincts telling her that he's not just a monster, but something more—something lost. She sees the torment in his eyes, the weight of a curse that has bound him for years, maybe longer. She knows, deep down, that he's not the enemy. The true enemy lies somewhere deeper, in the shadows of the past, where ancient forces stir.

Elara: (Softly) I'm not afraid of you.

Kieran flinches at her words, as though her compassion is a blow to his very soul. The moonlight glints off his sharp teeth as he fights to control the beast inside him. His eyes flicker between the wildness of the wolf and the human pain he can no longer hide.

Kieran: (Growling) You should be. You don't understand what I am. What I've become.

Elara steps closer, her gaze unwavering. She sees through the beast, through the curse, to the man who stands before her, tortured and alone.

Elara: (Firmly) I understand more than you think.

Kieran's body shudders, his muscles locking up as the transformation begins to take hold. His claws extend, and his face contorts with the strain of the change. He turns away, unable to face her, afraid of what he might become if he lets her in.

Kieran: (In agony) Please… go.

But Elara doesn't move. She's not afraid. She's drawn to him, not by the curse, but by something deeper, something that calls to her from the very core of her being. She reaches out a hand, as if offering him the one thing he has long since abandoned—hope.

Elara: (Gently) You don't have to be alone anymore. I'm not going anywhere.

In that moment, the air grows thick with tension. The howl of the wolf echoes once more, but it's softer now, less mournful. As if, for a fleeting moment, Kieran believes that maybe—just maybe—he's not beyond saving.

The Howl in the Dark

Scene 5: The Rising Moon

The transformation is complete. Kieran's eyes, wild and amber, fixate on Elara, his form now fully that of the beast. The moon above them is full, its light spilling across the clearing, bathing them in its cold glow.

Elara doesn't flinch. She stands her ground, the weight of the night pressing in around them, the mystery of the howl only deepening.

Kieran: (In a strained voice) You shouldn't have come.

But Elara doesn't answer. She simply watches him, her heart torn between fear and something else—something she can't name yet, but that she feels with every breath she takes. The night stretches on, filled with silence, save for the faint rustle of the wind through the trees and the soft thrum of Kieran's heartbeat, so close, yet so far away.

Two

The Stranger's Touch

Scene 1: The Silent Hour

The night wears on, shrouded in the thick mist that always comes after the full moon. The trees whisper in the wind, their long limbs swaying, casting strange shadows upon the earth. In the clearing, Elara stands alone, her heart racing as the echoes of Kieran's transformation reverberate in her mind. The beast is gone now, but she can still feel his presence, like an unshakable weight in the air.

She stands, her feet rooted to the ground, her eyes locked on the spot where Kieran stood only moments ago. The howl still lingers in the atmosphere, a reminder of the raw, desperate agony that had filled the night. But now, there is only silence—heavy, suffocating silence. She feels her pulse, steady and slow, as the cold night air bites at her skin.

The Stranger's Touch

Elara: (Softly, to herself) What is this place?

The words slip from her lips without thought. A question. A whisper. She wasn't sure what drew her to Ashgrove in the first place, but now that she was here, she couldn't deny that something deep inside her was pulling her toward the heart of the mystery. She knew she couldn't leave—not now. Not when she was so close to the answers.

She turns slowly, scanning the dark forest behind her. The trees seem to lean in, as though watching her every move. The air crackles with the strange energy that always seems to cling to the unknown. She can feel something moving—something or someone—just beyond the reach of her senses.

Elara: (Whispers) Kieran... Where are you?

A shadow shifts between the trees, too quick for her to see clearly. Her breath catches in her throat. She takes a cautious step forward, then another. Every nerve in her body is alert, every instinct telling her to run, yet something pulls her deeper into the woods.

She hears a rustle, like something brushing against the underbrush, and her heart leaps in her chest. She freezes, straining to hear.

A figure steps out from the shadows. The man is tall, his features sharp and striking, his eyes glowing with a faint, unnatural light. He is dressed in dark clothes, his movements fluid and deliberate. Elara's pulse quickens as she takes in his presence. There is something about him—something unsettling.

Stranger: (In a low, smooth voice) You shouldn't be here.

Elara's hand instinctively moves toward the dagger at her belt. The stranger's gaze meets hers, and something flickers in the depths of his eyes—a glimmer of recognition. Her fingers tighten around the hilt, though she knows it won't do much against a man who appears as otherworldly as he does.

Elara: (Voice trembling slightly) Who are you?

The stranger steps closer, his presence almost overwhelming, as though the very air around him bends to his will. His eyes never leave hers as he moves with an eerie grace. His voice, when he speaks again, is almost hypnotic.

Stranger: (Calmly) You've heard the howls, haven't you? The cry of the wolf. It's not just a sound, you know. It's a warning.

Elara's grip tightens on the dagger, but her curiosity outweighs her fear. She senses that this man knows more about the curse—and about Kieran—than she ever could have imagined.

Elara: (Challenging) A warning? From whom? And why are you here?

The stranger smiles, though it doesn't quite reach his eyes. There's something dark in his smile, something that makes the hairs on the back of Elara's neck stand on end. He takes another

The Stranger's Touch

step closer, his eyes flickering to her hand on the dagger before looking back into her eyes.

Stranger: (Quietly) I'm here because you've crossed a line. You've drawn the attention of something far darker than the beast you think you know. And you're not prepared for what comes next.

Elara feels the weight of his words, but she doesn't flinch. She has faced danger before, and she won't back down now. But still, there's a part of her that wonders: Who is this man? And why does he seem so familiar?

Elara: (Firmly) I'm not afraid of you.

Stranger: (Softly, almost pitying) You should be.

His words hang in the air like a warning bell. Before Elara can respond, a sudden gust of wind rushes through the clearing, throwing leaves into the air. The stranger's figure blurs for a moment, as if he's not entirely human. Elara blinks, and when she opens her eyes again, he's standing much closer, almost too close. His scent is strange, like damp earth and something more—something ancient.

Stranger: (In a low whisper) You think you know the wolf, but there's more to this town than you can see. You don't know what you've walked into. You don't know the darkness that lies beneath the surface.

Elara steps back, a chill crawling up her spine. The way he

speaks—there is no fear in his voice, only certainty, and it shakes her more than she cares to admit. She knows he's not lying. Whatever this man knows, it's not just about Kieran's curse—it's about something much older.

Elara: (Trying to steady her voice) What do you want from me?

Stranger: (With a hint of amusement) What do I want? You're the one who came looking for answers. Don't pretend you're not curious. You want to know what's behind the howls. You want to know what the curse really is. But be warned, child… Some truths are best left buried.

His words strike Elara to the core. She's been searching for answers, yes, but she never expected the cost to be so high. Her heart races, the weight of the unknown pressing down on her like a physical force. Still, she stands her ground.

Elara: (Defiantly) I'm not leaving until I understand what's happening here.

The stranger stares at her for a long moment, his eyes flicking toward the horizon where the moon hangs in the sky. A shift happens, subtle but unmistakable. His demeanor changes, his posture less threatening, more… resigned.

Stranger: (Sighing) You're more like him than you know. Stubborn. Determined. A fool, maybe. But it's not your fault. Not yet.

Elara frowns, confused. Kieran? What did he mean?

The Stranger's Touch

Elara: (Curiously) More like who? What do you mean?

Stranger: (Smiling faintly) You'll find out soon enough. Just remember—whatever you think you know about this town, about Kieran, it's only part of the story. The rest... it's darker than you can imagine.

The stranger's smile fades, and his expression becomes serious, even grave. He steps back, as if preparing to leave, but his eyes never leave Elara's. He studies her for a moment longer, as if weighing something in his mind.

Stranger: (Softly) Trust no one here. Not even him.

With that, he turns and disappears into the forest, vanishing as quickly as he had appeared. Elara stands in the clearing, her heart pounding, the weight of his warning pressing down on her like a thick fog. She's not sure what to make of him, but she knows one thing for certain: whatever secrets lie in Ashgrove, she's only just begun to scratch the surface.

Scene 2: Alone in the Dark

Elara stands alone in the clearing, the chill of the night creeping into her bones. She feels the tension in the air, the silence that has returned to the woods, broken only by the rustle of the wind through the leaves. Her mind races as she tries to make sense of the stranger's words. Who was he? What did he mean by "you're more like him than you know"?

She knows she needs to find Kieran, to understand the curse

that binds him. But the stranger's warning haunts her. She can't shake the feeling that she's stumbled into something far bigger, far more dangerous than she could have ever imagined. And now, she has no choice but to go deeper into the mystery.

Elara: (Whispers to herself) I'll find the truth. No matter what it takes.

As she turns to leave the clearing, a shiver runs down her spine. She doesn't know if it's the cold, the lingering presence of the stranger, or something else entirely. But she feels it—a presence, watching her from the shadows.

The darkness is deeper than she ever could have imagined.

Three

The Secret of the Howl

Scene 1: The Town of Ashgrove

The morning after the encounter with the stranger, Ashgrove appears as though it is trapped in time—its ancient buildings slouched in quiet decay, its streets empty, save for the occasional flicker of a figure disappearing behind a window or door. The town seems untouched by the world outside, as though the people here have long ago retreated from any hint of change. The fog still clings to the earth, heavy and oppressive, making the town feel suffocating.

Elara walks slowly through the cobbled streets, her eyes narrowed in thought. The encounter with the stranger still weighs heavily on her mind. She doesn't know what he meant by his words, nor the true nature of Kieran's curse, but the more she thinks about it, the more she senses that the town itself is hiding something—something that connects to the howls she's heard every night, and to the creature who had howled them.

She stops in front of an old inn, its weathered sign hanging by a single rusted chain. There's a strange pull that beckons her inside, an intuition telling her that she needs to speak to someone—someone who might know more about the curse that has claimed Kieran. She pushes open the door, the hinges creaking loudly in the silence of the morning.

Inside, the inn is dimly lit, the air thick with the scent of stale beer and old wood. A fire crackles softly in the hearth, its warmth almost a comfort against the chill that lingers outside. At the far end of the room, an old woman sits behind the bar, polishing a glass with a rag. Her eyes, though dull with age, are sharp as she watches Elara approach.

Innkeeper: (Gruffly) You look like someone who's searching for answers.

Elara nods slowly, her heart heavy with unspoken questions.

Elara: (Carefully) I heard the howls last night. The wolf's cry. I… I need to understand it. To understand why it happens.

The innkeeper sets down the glass and looks at Elara with a mixture of skepticism and something darker—something guarded.

Innkeeper: (With a low chuckle) The howls. Everyone who lives here hears them. Some ignore them. Some fear them. But

The Secret of the Howl

few know the truth of what they really are. You think you want the truth, girl, but the truth has a price.

Elara: (Determined) I'm not afraid of the truth.

The innkeeper's gaze sharpens, her lips tightening into a thin line. She studies Elara for a long moment before she finally nods, as if deciding something in her mind.

Innkeeper: (Softly) There's an old legend. A curse, passed down through the generations. It's not just the beast that howls, you know. The howl itself is a warning—a message from the past. And it's not just a man who turns into that wolf under the moon. It's a cycle, an endless cycle. Every full moon, the curse is renewed. Every night, it gets stronger. And the howl… the howl is a cry for help. But no one can hear it, except those who are meant to.

Elara listens closely, her heart thudding in her chest as the innkeeper's words settle into her mind.

Innkeeper: (Sighing) Years ago, before the town was built, there was a great battle. A battle between the ancient ones, creatures of the night who ruled over the land, and a dark power that sought to destroy them all. The creatures fought to protect the forest, the town, the lives of those who lived here. But the darkness was relentless. And in the end, one of the creatures—one of the great protectors—was cursed. His howls… they are a reminder of that lost battle. A reminder of a promise broken. A warning that the darkness will rise again, unless the curse is broken.

The Crying Wolf and the Darkest Night

Elara feels a shiver run down her spine, a coldness creeping into her bones as the innkeeper's words take root.

Elara: (Whispering) Kieran.

Innkeeper: (Nodding slowly) Yes. Kieran is the last of them. The last of the protectors. The one who carries the weight of the curse. Every full moon, he is forced to transform, forced to howl, to remind us all of the evil that still waits. And every time he howls, the darkness grows closer. He can't stop it. And neither can you.

Elara feels as if the air has been sucked from her lungs. The pieces are starting to fall into place—Kieran's curse, the howls, the mysterious stranger. But there's more. There's always more, isn't there?

Elara: (Voice steady) How do I stop it? How do I help him?

The innkeeper leans forward, her voice dropping to a whisper as she speaks.

Innkeeper: (Solemnly) To stop the curse, you must first understand it. And to understand it, you must go to the heart of the forest. The place where the battle was fought. The place where the curse was born. But be warned, girl. The forest isn't just a place. It's a living thing. A thing that watches, that listens. And those who go too deep may never come back.

Elara's mind races. The heart of the forest. The place where the battle was fought. She knows what she must do, even though the path ahead seems fraught with danger. Kieran's curse is tied to this place—this forest. And the only way to free him, to stop the howls, is to confront the darkness at its heart.

Elara: (Determined) I'll go. I'll find it. I'll find a way to break the curse.

The innkeeper looks at her, a faint smile tugging at her lips, but it's a smile tinged with something sad, something resigned.

Innkeeper: (Quietly) You may not like what you find, girl. But if you truly want to help him... you'll have to face the truth. And the truth... it's not always kind.

Scene 2: The Path into the Forest

That evening, as dusk falls over Ashgrove, Elara prepares herself for the journey. The innkeeper has given her little more than a warning and a direction—toward the heart of the forest. As the sun sinks below the horizon, the sky is painted in shades of purple and gold, but Elara hardly notices the beauty. Her thoughts are consumed with Kieran, with the curse, with the howls that still echo in her mind.

She walks toward the edge of the town, where the forest begins, its towering trees dark and foreboding against the evening sky. The wind picks up, carrying the scent of pine and earth, and Elara's senses sharpen. There's something waiting for her in those trees. Something ancient. Something that doesn't want to be found.

The Crying Wolf and the Darkest Night

The forest swallows her whole as she steps into the shadow of the trees. The path is narrow and winding, obscured by the thick underbrush and roots that claw at her feet. The air grows cooler with each step, the silence oppressive. The further she goes, the more the forest seems to close in around her. It feels as though the very earth beneath her feet is watching, waiting, listening.

Every rustle in the trees makes her jump. Every snap of a twig beneath her boot seems louder than the last. But she keeps going. She has no choice. The fate of Kieran, of Ashgrove, depends on her finding this heart of the forest. The place where the curse began.

As she presses forward, the light of the moon above her begins to dim, swallowed by the thick canopy of leaves above. The deeper she goes, the more oppressive the darkness becomes, until the forest is so black, so still, that it feels as if she's walking through a void.

And then she hears it. A distant cry. A howl. Kieran's howl.

It echoes through the trees, sharp and desperate, and Elara's heart lurches. She knows that sound. It's the sound of a man in agony, a soul trapped in an eternal cycle of pain.

But this time… it's different. The howl is not just a cry for help. It's a warning.

Elara pushes forward, her mind filled with fear and determination. She knows she is close. She can feel it. The heart of the forest is near. And with it, the answer to the curse that binds Kieran.

Scene 3: The Heart of the Forest

As Elara reaches the center of the forest, the air grows still. The trees form a circle around her, their trunks twisted and gnarled, as if shaped by some unseen force. In the center of the clearing stands an ancient stone altar, its surface covered in moss and blood-red markings. The moonlight spills across the altar, illuminating its eerie glow.

Elara approaches cautiously, her breath shallow. This is it. This is the heart of the forest. The place where the curse began. And the answers she seeks.

As she steps closer to the altar, the howl echoes again, louder this time, closer. The sound seems to come from all directions, as if the very forest is alive with the cry. Elara stands frozen, her heart pounding in her chest, as the darkness closes in around her.

Four

Whispers in the Wind

Scene 1: The Altar of Ashgrove

The air in the clearing is thick with an unnatural stillness. The moon hangs high above, its pale light casting an eerie glow over the ancient stone altar at the center of the circle of twisted trees. Elara stands before it, her breath shallow, her heart pounding in her chest. Every instinct tells her to turn back, to flee into the forest, but she can't. Not now. Not when she's so close to the answers she's been searching for.

The howl echoes again, louder this time, as if it's right behind her. It sends a jolt of fear through her spine, but she refuses to let it break her resolve. She needs to know what's happening to Kieran, why the curse that binds him has endured for so long. And more than that, she needs to understand the power that lurks within the forest—the darkness that seems to be growing stronger with each passing night.

Elara steps closer to the altar, the moss beneath her boots soft and damp, the stone cold beneath her fingertips. The air is heavy, laden with the scent of earth and decay. She runs her hand along the carvings etched into the stone, their meaning just beyond her understanding. The symbols are ancient, old beyond reckoning, and yet she feels a strange pull toward them—a sense of familiarity, as if she's seen them before, somewhere, somehow.

The howl comes again, but this time it is different. The sound shifts, changes, as if the very wind itself is carrying it. It's no longer just a cry of pain. It's a summons. A call. A plea that Elara feels deep in her bones.

Suddenly, the wind picks up, swirling around her, tossing her hair into her face. The trees groan and creak, their branches scraping against each other like the claws of some unseen predator. The atmosphere grows charged with an energy she can't explain, an energy that makes her skin crawl. She tries to steady herself, her heart racing, her mind screaming at her to leave. But she stands her ground, even as the howls grow louder, more frantic.

And then, as though in answer to her defiance, a voice whispers in the wind. The voice is faint at first, barely audible, but it grows louder, closer, until it's as though it's speaking directly to her.

The Crying Wolf and the Darkest Night

Voice: (Whispering, barely audible) Elara… Elara…

Her pulse quickens, and she looks around, her eyes wide, her body tense. There is no one here, no one but the wind and the trees. And yet, the voice is unmistakable—a low, guttural whisper that seems to come from the very air itself.

Voice: (Again, clearer) You're not alone. You never were.

Elara's breath catches in her throat. The voice is familiar, but she can't place it. It's as if she's heard it before, in a dream, in a memory she can't quite reach. Her eyes dart around the clearing, but there is no one. No one but the shadows and the wind.

The howl comes again, this time so close that Elara feels it vibrate through the ground beneath her feet. The wind shifts, and with it, the voice changes, morphing into something darker, something more sinister.

Voice: (Harsh, rasping) You don't know what you're walking into. You don't understand the weight of the curse.

Elara's heart races in her chest as she takes a step back, her hand instinctively reaching for the dagger at her side. The wind howls louder now, pulling at her hair and clothing, as though trying to drag her deeper into the forest. The voice seems to grow more insistent, more desperate.

Voice: (Urgent) You're too late… the darkness is already here.

Whispers in the Wind

Elara's mind is reeling, her thoughts racing as the wind swirls around her, pulling her deeper into the darkness of the clearing. She can't see the source of the voice, but she can feel it—feel it in the very air she breathes. The trees seem to bend closer, their branches stretching out like fingers, and she feels a sudden, overwhelming sense of being watched.

She turns in a panic, her eyes scanning the shadows, but still, there's nothing. Nothing but the whispering wind and the sound of her own breath. Her pulse races, and she feels the weight of the curse pressing down on her—an ancient, unseen force that seems to be closing in around her, tightening its grip.

Voice: (Whispering, pleading) The heart of the forest... it's not what you think. It's not just a place. It's a prison.

Elara's blood runs cold at the words. A prison? A place, yes, but a prison? She doesn't understand. She can't. But the voice seems to be pulling her toward the altar, toward the ancient carvings etched into the stone.

Voice: (Growling, dark) It's all connected. The howl... Kieran... the curse... it's all a part of the same cycle. You can't break it. You can't escape it.

Elara's hands shake as she steps back, her breath coming in ragged gasps. She can't stay here. She can't. She has to find Kieran, has to stop the curse before it consumes him completely. But the voice won't let her go. The wind won't let her escape.

The trees groan, and the ground beneath her feet shifts, as

though the very earth is alive, pulling her deeper into the heart of the forest. Elara stumbles back, her heart racing as the shadows close in around her. She can't breathe, can't think, only run.

But she's trapped. The path she came from is gone, swallowed by the darkness that now surrounds her. The howl comes again, louder this time, filled with pain and desperation. And with it, the voice calls out once more, this time clearer than ever before.

Voice: (Raging, furious) You should never have come. Now you'll suffer the same fate. You'll become part of the curse. Part of the cycle.

Elara feels the ground beneath her feet tremble, and the trees begin to bend inward, their branches curling like tendrils. She looks around in a panic, her mind whirling. The air is thick with the stench of decay, the weight of centuries pressing down on her shoulders. She can feel it now—the pull of something ancient, something evil, drawing her toward the altar. And the whispers in the wind grow louder, more insistent.

Voice: (Softly, in her ear) You can't escape, Elara. No one ever has.

Her pulse races, her breath coming faster now as she turns toward the altar, the ancient stone in front of her. The carvings on the altar seem to glow with an otherworldly light, as though the very stone is alive. The wind picks up, howling around her, and Elara feels herself being drawn closer, pulled toward the stone by an invisible force.

Voice: (Screaming, final) You were never meant to find the truth.

Elara stumbles toward the altar, her hand outstretched, her fingers trembling as she reaches for the stone. The howl crescendos, filling the air, and for a moment, everything goes silent. She can feel the pull of the curse, the weight of the darkness pressing down on her like a vice.

But just as her fingers touch the stone, a hand shoots out from the shadows, grabbing her wrist with a strength that takes her breath away. Elara gasps, spinning around to see the figure standing behind her.

It's Kieran.

His eyes are wild, his face contorted in pain and desperation. He's no longer the man she saw last night—he's the wolf now, a beast trapped in a man's body, his form twisted by the curse. His grip on her wrist is unyielding, and she can feel the heat of his touch, the pulse of something unnatural flowing through him.

Kieran: (Urgently) You shouldn't have come here, Elara. You have no idea what you're dealing with.

The wind howls again, and the trees groan in response, their branches snapping in the wind. Elara looks into Kieran's eyes, fear and confusion clouding her thoughts. She wants to pull away, to run, but she can't.

Kieran: (Desperate, his voice cracking) The forest knows you're here. And it's not going to let you leave.

The whispers in the wind grow louder, more frantic, as the shadows around them shift, as if they are alive, waiting.

Five

The Full Moon's Grip

Scene 1: The Heart of the Forest

The wind howls through the trees, bending and snapping the branches like fragile twigs. The darkness presses in from all sides, heavy with the weight of an unseen force. Elara's breath catches in her throat as she stands frozen, caught in the grip of Kieran's hand. His eyes—wild, desperate, pleading—lock onto hers, a mixture of fear and sorrow flickering within their depths.

Kieran: (Low, strained) You shouldn't be here, Elara. You don't understand what you're walking into.

Elara's pulse pounds in her ears, her fingers tingling with the touch of his skin. She wants to pull away, but his grip tightens, as though he's holding onto her for dear life. The howl of the wind drowns out everything else, and for a moment, the only sound in the world is the frantic beating of her own heart.

Elara: (Breathless) Kieran… What is this? What's happening? Why does it feel like the forest itself is alive?

Kieran's expression hardens, his jaw clenching in pain as he struggles to find the right words. The ground beneath them trembles, and the wind picks up again, causing the trees to creak and groan like ancient, wounded creatures.

Kieran: (Grimly) The forest… It's not just the place where the curse was born. It's part of it. It's tied to me. To the moon. The howl… the pain you hear at night… it's all connected. The full moon, Elara… it's when the curse is at its strongest. It's when it takes hold of me. And it won't let go until it's done with me.

He pulls her closer, his grip almost desperate, as though afraid she'll slip through his fingers and disappear into the night. Elara's breath catches in her throat as she meets his gaze. The weight of his words sinks in, and she can feel the pull of something dark—something ancient and unrelenting—gripping at her heart.

Kieran: (Hoarsely) I've tried to fight it. For years. But when the moon rises… it's like I'm no longer myself. The beast takes over, and I can't control it. I can't stop it from… hurting people.

Elara's eyes widen, and she feels a cold shiver crawl down her spine. She's heard the stories—the rumors, the whispers about the creature that haunts the town—but hearing Kieran speak of it, seeing the pain in his eyes, makes the truth hit her like a physical blow.

Elara: (Softly) Kieran, you're not a monster. You don't have to be.

Kieran shakes his head, his lips trembling as he speaks. His eyes flicker toward the altar, and Elara follows his gaze. The stone altar looms before them, its ancient carvings glowing faintly in the moonlight. The air around them crackles with a strange energy, and Elara can feel the pulse of the curse vibrating through her chest.

Kieran: (Bitterly) You don't understand, Elara. The curse doesn't care about who I am or who I want to be. It only cares about its own hunger. Its need to destroy, to feed on the very essence of the night. The full moon... it's its feeding time. And every time it rises, the curse grows stronger. More violent. More insatiable.

He releases her wrist, his hands trembling at his sides as if the mere act of speaking about the curse is too much to bear. He steps back, his gaze dark and haunted as he watches the moon rise higher in the sky. The night seems to stretch out before them, endless and full of impending dread.

Kieran: (Sighing) I thought I could protect you, Elara. I thought I could keep you safe. But now... now you're involved. The curse... it's already found you.

Elara's heart skips a beat. She takes a step forward, her eyes wide with disbelief.

Elara: (Frantic) What do you mean? I'm not part of this! I don't want to be part of this!

Kieran's voice is low and pained as he speaks, his words hanging in the air like a cold, heavy fog.

Kieran: (Gravely) You don't get to choose, Elara. Once the forest knows you're here, once it knows your name... it never lets go. The curse binds you to it. It binds you to me. And now... now that you've come this far, it won't let you leave. It will consume you, just like it's consumed me.

Elara takes a step back, her pulse racing, her mind whirling. She doesn't want to believe him. She can't. But the fear in his eyes—the same fear that has clawed at her own heart since she arrived in Ashgrove—tells her that he's not lying. That the darkness is real. That the curse is real.

Elara: (Shaken) I won't let it take me, Kieran. I won't let it take you either.

Kieran shakes his head, his face twisted with anguish.

Kieran: (Harshly) It's already too late. You don't understand. The full moon's grip is already on me. The beast... it's already waking up. It's too strong. There's nothing I can do to stop it now.

The wind howls louder, a guttural, mournful sound that echoes

The Full Moon's Grip

through the clearing. The trees seem to bend and twist, their branches reaching out like fingers, as if trying to claim Elara and Kieran both. The air grows colder, and Elara feels the full weight of the curse pressing in on her, suffocating her with its dark, malevolent power.

Suddenly, Kieran stumbles back, his breath ragged, his body shuddering as if he's fighting against an invisible force. His eyes flash with panic, and for a moment, Elara sees the flicker of the beast inside him—something primal, something terrifying that she can't fully comprehend.

Kieran: (Desperate, panting) It's... it's happening. I can't hold it back much longer.

Elara reaches for him, her heart aching with helplessness as she watches him struggle against the transformation. His body twists and contorts, his muscles bulging as the curse takes hold. She can see the pain in his face—the anguish of a man caught between two worlds, struggling to hold onto his humanity as the beast inside him threatens to tear him apart.

Elara: (Pleading) Kieran, please! You have to fight it! You have to—

Kieran's body convulses violently, his spine arching as a guttural growl escapes his throat. His eyes flash an unnatural yellow, and his hands curl into claws, the transformation almost complete. Elara stumbles back, fear gripping her chest as she watches in horror.

The Crying Wolf and the Darkest Night

Kieran: (Gravely) I… I can't, Elara. I'm sorry. I'm sorry…

With a final, anguished cry, Kieran collapses to his knees, his body convulsing as the transformation takes hold. His face contorts, elongating into the form of the wolf, the beast he's been cursed to become with each full moon. Elara watches in horror, her breath catching in her throat as the creature before her rises to its full, terrifying height.

The wolf—Kieran—is now fully transformed. Its eyes glow with a feral intensity, its body sleek and muscular, covered in thick fur. The air around them crackles with power as the beast howls again, the sound reverberating through the trees, shaking the ground beneath them. Elara feels the forest itself tremble in response.

But despite the creature's fearsome appearance, there's a flicker of recognition in its eyes. The same eyes that were once human, once Kieran's. And in that fleeting moment, Elara understands—the man she's come to care for is still there, trapped within the beast. But for how long?

The beast turns toward her, its gaze intense, hungry. Elara takes a step back, her heart racing in her chest. She doesn't know if the creature before her will remember who she is—if it will recognize her as the woman who has come to save him, or as another victim to tear apart. But one thing is clear: she's running out of time.

The full moon's grip has claimed him completely.

Six

The Curse Unveiled

Scene 1: The Blood-Soaked Moon

The full moon hangs high in the sky, its pale light bathing the clearing in a cold, unnatural glow. The forest seems to hold its breath, the very air trembling with the power that courses through it. Elara stands frozen, her heart hammering in her chest, her eyes wide with disbelief as she watches Kieran's transformation unfold. The beast he's become is terrifying—its eyes burning with an ancient rage, its muscles rippling under its dark fur. Yet, beneath the monster's visage, there's a flicker of the man she's come to know, a fleeting trace of humanity trapped within.

The wolf—Kieran's beastly form—stares at her with a gaze so intense that it feels as though it's reaching into her very soul. For a moment, Elara feels as though the ground beneath her feet is slipping away, as though the darkness is closing in on her from all sides. The howling wind picks up, swirling around them like a vortex, and she can feel the weight of something ancient, something deeply cursed, pressing down on her chest.

But then, Kieran's voice—low and strained—breaks through the madness, his words barely recognizable through the guttural growls that rip from his throat.

Kieran: (Snarling, desperate) Elara… run… now!

His voice is still Kieran's, but distorted, torn between the man and the beast. Elara hesitates, her body rooted to the spot as she watches him, her mind racing. She's heard the stories, the rumors, about the curse that plagues him, but nothing—nothing had prepared her for the raw terror she feels now. The forest is alive, and Kieran is its prisoner. But the voice within him—the human part of him—is fighting, struggling against the curse that threatens to consume him completely.

Elara: (Shaking, her voice trembling) I'm not leaving you, Kieran! I'm not running! I'll help you! I swear I will!

Kieran growls again, his body convulsing with a mix of pain and rage. His claws scrape against the earth, leaving deep gouges in the soil as he struggles against the transformation that continues to claim him. His chest rises and falls with heavy breaths, each one filled with a deep, bone-shaking agony. Elara can see it now—the terror in his eyes. The beast is stronger than ever, but there's a flicker of Kieran still fighting inside.

The Curse Unveiled

Kieran: (Faintly, through clenched teeth) The curse... Elara... it's not just me... it's this forest... it's... it's not just the full moon...

Elara's heart skips a beat. The weight of his words crashes into her like a wave, drowning her in its implications. The curse isn't just a part of Kieran—it's tied to the forest itself, to the very land that surrounds them. The howl, the pain, the relentless grip of the moon... it's all part of something much larger, much darker than she could have ever imagined.

Before she can respond, the beast that Kieran has become lets out a deafening roar, its massive form shaking the ground beneath their feet. The earth trembles as though it, too, is caught in the grip of something ancient and powerful. Elara stumbles backward, her body tense with fear as the wolf steps toward her, its eyes glowing with an unnatural intensity.

But just as the beast lunges, Kieran's voice—broken and desperate—cuts through the air, a cry that seems to echo from deep within his soul.

Kieran: (In a low, tortured voice) Elara, you have to listen... you have to know the truth.

The wolf pauses mid-step, its claws digging into the ground as if fighting against the force that's driving it forward. The moment of hesitation is fleeting, but in it, Elara sees a glimpse of Kieran—trapped, struggling within the beast. Her breath catches in her throat, and she takes a cautious step closer to him, her eyes searching his for any sign of recognition.

The Crying Wolf and the Darkest Night

Elara: (Urgently) What truth, Kieran? What do you mean?

Kieran's eyes flicker with a deep, unfathomable sorrow as he stares at her. He doesn't answer immediately, his body writhing as if the very act of speaking is a struggle. The wind howls again, and the trees around them seem to shake with an ancient, primal power.

Kieran: (Weakly) The curse… it wasn't just placed on me. It was placed on all of us. On this entire town. Ashgrove wasn't always like this. The forest… it wasn't always cursed. But something happened. Something dark, something ancient… and it corrupted the land. It made the full moon its time to feed, its time to turn the living into the monstrous. It made me its prisoner… and now… now it wants you, too.

Elara's breath catches in her throat as the weight of Kieran's words settles over her like a shroud. The curse isn't just his burden to bear—it's a curse that has infected everything in Ashgrove, from the very earth beneath their feet to the hearts of the people who live there. The wind picks up, howling through the trees, as if the forest itself is reacting to the revelation.

Elara: (Whispering) Why… why did it choose you, Kieran? Why did it choose this town?

Kieran lets out a low growl, his eyes flickering between human desperation and wolfish rage. His claws scrape the earth again, and his body shudders as the transformation continues to tighten its grip on him.

The Curse Unveiled

Kieran: (Choking) It wasn't supposed to be like this. The forest... it used to be a place of peace, a place where we could all live together. But greed... power... the desire to control the land, to take from it... it all changed things. An ancient evil... something older than time itself... it was awakened. And it began to feed on the people, to twist them into something unrecognizable. It fed on fear, on darkness. And I... I was its first victim.

Elara's heart aches as she watches Kieran, her hand trembling as she reaches toward him. She can see it now—the pain in his eyes, the suffering he's endured for so long, trapped between the man he once was and the beast he's forced to become every month. The curse is a living, breathing thing, a force so powerful that it has consumed not only Kieran but the very land itself.

Elara: (Softly, with understanding) And now... it wants me. It wants us both.

Kieran nods, his body twitching as if the words are physically painful for him to say.

Kieran: (Hushed) Yes. The moment you set foot in Ashgrove, the curse recognized you. It knows who you are. And it knows what you mean to me. It wants to claim you, Elara. It wants to bind you to it, to make you a part of the cycle. It's never going to let you go. Not until it has everything it wants.

Elara's breath catches in her throat as the weight of his words hits her like a physical blow. She wants to scream, to run, to

The Crying Wolf and the Darkest Night

escape the suffocating grip of the forest, but she can't. She's already too deep into this. And Kieran—he's not just a victim; he's a part of this curse, a part of this twisted fate. She can't leave him, not now, not when she knows the truth.

Elara: (Fiercely) No. I won't let it take me. I won't let it take you. We'll fight it. Together.

Kieran's eyes flicker with something like hope, a brief spark of humanity before the wolf takes over again. He growls, his body shaking with the strain of holding onto his human side. The transformation is nearing its completion, and the beast within him is rising again, relentless and all-consuming.

Kieran: (Grimly) It's too late for me. You can't fight this alone. I'm… I'm already lost.

The forest seems to respond to Kieran's words, its shadows thickening, its branches reaching out like claws. The howl of the wind grows louder, filling the air with a sense of impending doom.

Elara takes a step closer, her heart aching with the weight of his words, but her resolve is firm. She can't lose him—not now, not when they've just begun to uncover the truth.

Elara: (Whispering) No, Kieran. We're not lost. We're not finished. I won't let you go.

The howl of the wolf rises again, and Elara braces herself for the fight of her life. The curse is unveiled, and its grip is tightening.

The Curse Unveiled

But she's not giving up. Not without a fight.

Seven

The Midnight Duel

Scene 1: The Heart of the Forest

The full moon has reached its apex, bathing the clearing in an eerie, silvery glow. The air is thick with tension, and the forest, once alive with the hum of night creatures, now stands deathly silent. Elara stands at the edge of the clearing, her breath steady but her heart racing in her chest. Kieran—the beast that has become him—circles the perimeter, his massive form moving with a predatory grace that sends shivers down her spine. His eyes, glowing with an unnatural yellow light, are fixed on her, tracking her every move. Every breath feels like a life-or-death decision.

Kieran's voice—rough and strained—breaks the silence, low and guttural as he speaks.

The Midnight Duel

Kieran: (With a growl) Elara, you don't understand. The curse… it's more than just a transformation. It's a duel—an eternal battle for control. The beast inside me, it doesn't just want to kill. It wants to destroy everything. And tonight… tonight, it won't stop until it has everything. Everything I love.

Elara stands her ground, her pulse hammering in her throat. She can feel the weight of his words, the desperation and agony laced within them. Kieran—the man she's come to know, the man she believes is still inside the beast—speaks to her, pleading for understanding. But she's not sure if there's any humanity left to save.

Elara: (Steady) I don't care about the curse, Kieran. I care about you. You've been fighting this for so long. I can help you fight it. I can—

Kieran lets out a vicious snarl, cutting her off. His eyes flash dangerously, and he lunges toward her with the speed of a predator. Elara barely has time to react before the beast is upon her, its claws swiping through the air, tearing at the earth with the force of a storm. She stumbles back, her heart in her throat as the wolf growls, a sound like thunder in the stillness of the night.

Kieran: (With a growl, strained) This is not a fight you can win, Elara. This is my battle—my burden. You can't understand the strength of the curse, the pull of the beast. I won't let it take you down with me. I won't.

Elara's mind races. Her instincts scream at her to run, to escape while she still can. But her body won't move. She's rooted to the spot, her eyes locked onto Kieran's, seeing the struggle in his gaze. She knows he's still in there, buried deep beneath the rage of the wolf. And she's not leaving him. Not like this.

Elara: (Softly, with determination) I'm not afraid of you, Kieran. You're not just the beast. You're the man I've come to care for. And I won't abandon you.

The wolf pauses, a flicker of hesitation crossing its wild, glowing eyes. For a moment, Elara sees the faintest trace of the man Kieran used to be. But the beast within him is too strong, too hungry. With a roar, the wolf lunges again, its fangs bared, its claws like razors.

Elara leaps backward, narrowly avoiding the strike, and her heart races as she takes a step toward the altar—the ancient stone altar in the center of the clearing. She's heard the legends, the rumors that the altar holds power, that it's tied to the curse that has plagued Ashgrove for centuries. She doesn't know if it's a myth or if it will truly help her in this fight, but she's willing to try anything.

As she reaches the altar, Kieran follows, his massive form moving like a shadow, his glowing eyes never leaving her. He's gaining on her, his growls shaking the earth beneath their feet. Elara feels the forest closing in, the trees bending toward her as if they, too, are part of the curse, drawn to the confrontation. The night air is thick with energy, an electric charge that crackles between them.

The Midnight Duel

Elara reaches for the altar's surface, her fingers brushing against the cold stone. The carvings etched into it pulse with a faint light, an eerie glow that sends a jolt of energy through her fingertips. Her eyes widen as she realizes the power in the stone—it's ancient, it's primal, and it's connected to the curse in ways she can't yet understand.

Elara: (To herself, breathless) There's power here... power I can use.

Before she can fully process the thought, Kieran is upon her again, his claws raking through the air with terrifying precision. Elara dodges to the side, her body moving on instinct, but the force of the wolf's strike sends her sprawling to the ground. Pain flashes through her side as she crashes into the earth, her breath knocked out of her. She scrambles to her feet, her heart racing as she faces Kieran once more.

Kieran's eyes are wide with hunger, his breath coming in ragged gasps. The beast is winning, its control slipping from his grasp. His human side is buried, suffocated beneath the beast's primal instincts. Elara knows this is her only chance. She can't wait any longer. She can't hold back.

Elara: (Yelling, with strength) Kieran! Listen to me! You're not lost! You're not gone! You're still in there! Fight it!

For a moment, Kieran freezes. His claws, poised to strike, waver in the air as he struggles against the wolf's influence. The human side of him flickers in his eyes, his lips curling in an almost anguished grimace as he fights for control. But then—

just as quickly—his body jerks forward, the beast surging back into control. He roars in fury, a deafening, guttural sound that reverberates through the clearing.

Kieran: (Raging) You don't understand! I can't control it! I—

Before he can finish, Elara steps forward, her hands raised toward the altar, and she calls out the words she doesn't fully understand. The energy in the air shifts, crackling like lightning, and the stone beneath her hands glows brighter, casting a pale, otherworldly light across the clearing. The power of the altar, ancient and untapped for so long, surges through her, and she feels it connect with the very heartbeat of the land itself.

Elara: (Commanding) I won't let the curse win! I won't let you go, Kieran!

The energy of the altar pulses through her, and the air around them crackles with power. Kieran howls, his body convulsing as the wolf fights against the force she's unleashing. The beast is struggling, its strength pushing against the power she's drawing from the altar, but Elara's will is stronger. She feels the pull of something ancient, something that binds them both together. She can feel Kieran, his humanity still there, still fighting within the wolf. The connection between them is undeniable, and it's this connection—this bond—that gives her the strength to push back the curse.

The forest trembles as Elara's power reaches its peak, and Kieran stumbles, his body jerking as if caught between two

The Midnight Duel

worlds. The wolf's form wavers, its claws retracting slightly as the human side of him claws its way to the surface. For a brief moment, Elara sees Kieran in his eyes—human, vulnerable, and terrified.

Kieran: (Weakly, gasping) Elara... help me... please...

Elara's heart breaks as she watches him struggle, his body wracked with pain. She takes a step forward, reaching out her hand to him, her voice gentle but filled with determination.

Elara: (Softly) I'm here, Kieran. I'm not going anywhere.

But just as she reaches for him, the wolf surges forward again, and with a deafening roar, it lunges. Elara barely has time to react before Kieran's massive form slams into her, knocking her to the ground. The beast snarls, its fangs bared, its claws raking through the air as it pins her down.

Kieran's voice—broken, desperate—pierces through the chaos.

Kieran: (Pleading) You don't understand... you can't save me. It's too late. The duel is already over...

The wolf rears back, ready to strike, but Elara's grip tightens on the altar, and with one last, desperate cry, she channels everything she has into the ancient power beneath her hands. The ground shakes violently as the force of the curse meets the power of the altar in an explosive clash. The wolf recoils, its body jerking as if caught in an invisible force, and with one final, agonizing howl, it collapses to the ground.

The Crying Wolf and the Darkest Night

For a brief, breathless moment, silence falls over the clearing. The air is still, the wind holding its breath as the moonlight bathes the scene in a cold, quiet glow. Elara lies on the ground, her body aching, but her heart pounding in her chest as she waits for something—anything—to happen.

And then, slowly, painfully, Kieran's human form emerges from the depths of the wolf. His eyes are wild, filled with confusion and fear, but they are his eyes. His breath comes in short, ragged gasps as he pushes himself to his knees, the weight of the curse heavy on him.

Kieran: (Weakly, trembling) Elara… I…

Elara rushes to him, her hands trembling as she reaches out to touch his face, her heart swelling with relief and fear in equal measure.

Elara: (Softly, relieved) You're still here. You're still you.

Kieran looks at her, his eyes haunted, filled with an ancient sorrow as he reaches for her hand. The curse may not be broken, but for now, they've won a single, fragile victory.

Kieran: (Whispering) But for how long, Elara? For how long until the beast comes back?

Eight

A Night of Shadows

Scene 1: The Tides of Darkness

The clearing is silent now, the battle between the man and the beast momentarily subsided. The full moon looms overhead, a cold, watchful eye that casts its pale light over the scene. Kieran's form is slumped on the ground, his body trembling with exhaustion, his eyes dull with the weight of what he's just endured. Elara kneels beside him, her fingers gently brushing against his skin, checking for any signs of injury. Her heart beats wildly, still not fully understanding what just transpired, but knowing that the moment of peace they have now will not last long.

The wind stirs the leaves in the trees, sending a shiver through the air. A distant howl—sharp and cruel—echoes through the forest, a reminder that the night is far from over. The darkness is alive, and Elara knows that they are not alone.

Elara: (Softly, with fear) It's not over, is it? This... this peace... it won't last.

Kieran lifts his head, his expression weary, haunted. His eyes flicker to the moon, his body tense with the very realization she speaks. The darkness around them seems to pulse, to breathe, as if it's waiting for something, something that's about to come.

Kieran: (Grimly) No. It won't last. The curse... it doesn't end with just one battle. It's woven into the very fabric of this land. It's always watching. And it's always waiting.

Elara pulls herself up, her gaze searching the edges of the clearing, but the shadows are deep, too deep, curling like living things. The trees bend and sway, the darkness between them shifting as though the very forest is alive, aware of their presence. And then, she sees it—a figure, barely a silhouette, standing at the edge of the clearing. Tall and menacing, its form cloaked in shadow. Elara's breath catches in her throat, her body going cold.

Elara: (Whispering) Who's there?

Kieran's eyes snap open, his body immediately reacting to the threat. He stands shakily, his muscles tense as he scans the perimeter, his senses heightened. The figure moves forward, slowly, methodically. Its movements are smooth, almost unnatural, as it steps into the moonlight.

A Night of Shadows

Kieran: (Hissing) Stay back, Elara. It's not safe.

The figure steps forward, and Elara feels a chill run down her spine. It's a man—tall, his face hidden beneath the cloak of shadows. But there's something about him, something in the way he moves that sends a chill crawling down her back. There's no ordinary man who can step out of the shadows like that.

The figure speaks, his voice smooth, like silk sliding over glass.

Figure: (Low, dark) So, this is how it ends, Kieran. With a woman at your side, thinking she can save you. How quaint.

Elara steps forward, her hands clenched into fists, her heart pounding in her chest. She doesn't know who this man is, but the disdain in his voice is enough to fuel the fire in her veins.

Elara: (Defiantly) Who are you? What do you want with us?

The figure chuckles, a low, rumbling sound that fills the air with an almost predatory amusement. He steps closer, his eyes glowing faintly in the moonlight, piercing through the darkness like twin shards of ice.

Figure: (Darkly) I am the one who keeps the balance. The one who watches over the curse. The one who ensures it never ends. You might call me the Keeper. And you, my dear, have stepped into a world of shadows that you cannot escape. You can't save him. You can't save yourself.

The Crying Wolf and the Darkest Night

Elara's breath catches in her throat as the figure's words sink in. The Keeper. The one who keeps the curse alive. Her gaze flickers to Kieran, whose eyes are wide with recognition and fear. He steps back, his hands shaking as the weight of the words sinks in.

Kieran: (With a harsh whisper) No… no. You shouldn't be here. I… I've tried to stop it. I've tried to destroy the curse.

The Keeper smiles, his lips curling in a twisted mockery of amusement. He steps closer to Kieran, his presence oppressive, suffocating. The air seems to grow heavier with each step he takes, the ground beneath their feet trembling as if it, too, is afraid.

Keeper: (Mockingly) You think you've fought it? You think you've escaped it? No, Kieran. You're just a puppet, bound to the strings of the curse. It doesn't matter how many times you fight. It doesn't matter how many times you struggle. You will never be free.

Elara feels a cold terror spreading through her veins, but she refuses to let it consume her. She looks at Kieran, whose face is pale, his eyes full of defeat. He's been fighting this curse for so long, but she won't let him give in. Not now. Not when she knows there's still hope.

Elara: (To Kieran, firmly) Don't listen to him. You're not a puppet. You're a man. And you can still fight this.

Kieran's eyes flicker to her, the briefest flash of recognition

A Night of Shadows

before the Keeper steps forward again, his eyes locked on Elara.

Keeper: (Mockingly) Oh, how sweet. You think love will save him? You think the power of your feelings will end centuries of suffering? You are fooling yourselves.

The Keeper raises his hand, and the air around them begins to twist, to warp. The shadows stretch like tendrils, curling toward Kieran and Elara, closing in on them from every direction. Elara feels the air grow thick with a choking presence, as if the forest itself is alive and watching them, waiting for something to happen.

Kieran: (Growling, to the Keeper) Stop this! I won't let you take her.

The Keeper laughs softly, the sound chilling in its finality.

Keeper: (Darkly) You don't have a choice. You've already lost. The curse has you. And now… now it has her, too.

The shadows close in, wrapping around them, pressing against their skin like an invisible weight. Elara gasps, trying to break free, but the darkness is relentless, suffocating. Her heart races, her mind frantic. This isn't just a fight for survival. It's a fight for Kieran's soul, and her own. And the Keeper… the Keeper will stop at nothing to see them both fall.

Kieran steps forward, his body trembling, his eyes filled with anguish and determination. He knows the truth of the Keeper's words, knows the curse has been a part of him for so long. But

Elara's voice breaks through the darkness, a beacon of light in the suffocating shadows.

Elara: (Shouting, with a cry) Kieran! Fight! Don't give in!

The words seem to pierce through the shadows, and for a moment, the darkness falters. The shadows waver, and Kieran's form stiffens as though he's drawing on a power deep within himself. His muscles tense, his eyes flash with a wild, desperate light, and he roars—louder, more powerful than before. The shadows shudder as his voice breaks through them like a wave crashing against the shore.

Kieran: (Fiercely) I will not be a prisoner! Not anymore!

With a violent movement, Kieran throws himself into the darkness, pushing against the tendrils that are wrapping around him. The Keeper's smile falters as the force of Kieran's will pushes back the shadows, but the figure is not yet defeated. The battle is far from over.

Keeper: (Sneering) Foolish child. You think you can fight me? You are nothing but a fragment of what you once were.

The shadows lash out, striking at Kieran and Elara, but they refuse to back down. The battle rages between them, a clash of wills, of light against dark. Elara can feel the pull of the shadows, the suffocating grip of the curse, but she stands strong. She won't let Kieran lose himself—not when she's so close to helping him escape this nightmare.

A Night of Shadows

Kieran fights the darkness, his body wracked with the strain of holding onto his humanity. The Keeper's presence is overwhelming, but Elara can see it now—Kieran's resolve, his refusal to be consumed by the curse. The power of his defiance is enough to push back the darkness, to break through the Keeper's hold, even if only for a moment.

Elara: (Urgently) Kieran, we have to finish this. We can't let him win!

Kieran nods, his breath ragged, but his eyes are steady, determined. He knows this is their last chance. If they don't defeat the Keeper now, the curse will consume them both.

With a final, desperate roar, Kieran thrusts forward, his will unyielding, and the Keeper's shadowed form begins to fade, retreating into the darkness from which it came. But as the figure vanishes, the air crackles with a sense of finality, and Elara knows that this battle is far from over. The Keeper may have been pushed back, but the darkness is always waiting, always watching.

Nine

The Rising Darkness

Scene 1: The Calm Before the Storm

The clearing is still. Kieran and Elara stand at the center of the deserted forest, bathed in the light of the fading moon. The battle they fought moments before seems distant, almost unreal. But the heavy, oppressive silence that follows their victory over the Keeper hangs in the air like a storm waiting to break. Kieran stands motionless, his eyes fixed on the ground, as if tethered to a memory he cannot escape. Elara watches him, her heart heavy with the weight of what they've just endured.

Elara: (Quietly) Kieran… What now?

Kieran doesn't answer immediately. His eyes are lost, his body slack as though the fight has drained him of everything he had

The Rising Darkness

left to give. He's trembling, not from the cold, but from the lingering shadow of the curse that gnaws at his soul.

Kieran: (Whispering, almost to himself) It's not over. It can't be. The Keeper... he was just a fragment of something much worse. The darkness... it's rising again.

Elara takes a step toward him, her hand brushing against his. She can feel the tension in his body, the quiet storm of emotions brewing beneath the surface. She knows he's not just talking about the Keeper—he's talking about himself, about the curse that binds him to the night. But she also knows that they can't stand still any longer. The darkness is out there, waiting for them.

Elara: (Firmly) We have to keep moving. Whatever this is... we'll face it together. We've already come this far.

Kieran turns his head, his eyes meeting hers. They're filled with a sadness that cuts through her. The darkness isn't just external—it's a battle he fights within himself every single day. But she refuses to let that be the end. Not after everything they've been through.

Kieran: (Quietly) You don't understand. You don't know what it feels like to be hunted by your own soul. To be a prisoner of something that was never your choice. The full moon is just the beginning. The curse... it calls to me, Elara. It wants me. And it will take everything. It always does.

Elara's heart clenches at his words, but she shakes her head, determined.

Elara: (Softly) I don't care what it takes. We'll find a way to stop it. I promise.

Kieran gazes at her for a long moment, searching her face as though looking for something he's not sure he believes in. Then, without warning, he turns away, his eyes returning to the darkened horizon. The trees shift in the wind, casting strange, jagged shadows across the ground. The world feels too quiet, too still. The forest feels like it's holding its breath.

Kieran: (Harshly) The darkness doesn't wait for promises. It waits for weakness. And it finds it, no matter how much you fight.

Elara watches him, her heart aching for him, but she refuses to let him succumb to despair. She steps forward, placing a hand gently on his shoulder, grounding him with her touch. She doesn't have the answers, but she knows one thing for certain—they can't give up. Not now.

Elara: (Steadfastly) I'm not giving up on you, Kieran. Not now, not ever.

He closes his eyes, letting out a long breath, as though the weight of the world rests on his shoulders. The silence stretches between them, thick and heavy, until the stillness is broken by a sudden, distant howl—sharp, jagged, and filled with malice. The sound slices through the air, reverberating across the forest like an omen of something darker, something worse.

The Rising Darkness

Kieran's body stiffens, his eyes snapping open. He whirls around, his gaze scanning the surrounding darkness as if expecting to see the source of the howl appear from the shadows.

Kieran: (Urgently) We have to move. Now.

Elara doesn't hesitate. She knows there's no time to waste. Without another word, she follows Kieran as he leads them deeper into the forest, his senses alert, his body tense. The howl echoes again, closer this time, and then again—louder, more insistent. It's a call to arms, a signal that the darkness is stirring.

Scene 2: The Gathering Storm

The forest seems to pulse with a life of its own as they make their way through the trees, their footsteps silent on the soft earth beneath them. Every shadow feels like it's watching them, waiting. The air grows colder with each passing moment, and the wind carries with it the faint scent of decay, of something ancient and forgotten.

Elara's breath comes in short, quick bursts, her heart pounding in her chest. She can feel the weight of Kieran's presence beside her, his every movement a silent promise that they are in this together. But the tension in his shoulders tells her everything she needs to know—something is coming. And it won't be easy to face.

Elara: (Breathlessly) Kieran, what is it? What's out there?

Kieran doesn't answer right away. His eyes flicker toward the sky, the full moon now hanging low and heavy above them, casting a sickly light over the landscape. His gaze darkens as though the moon itself is a harbinger of the darkness that's creeping closer.

Kieran: (Grimly) It's them. The beasts. The ones who've been hunting me for years. The curse has always been tied to the bloodline. And when the full moon rises, they answer the call.

Elara's heart sinks. The "beasts" Kieran speaks of—she's heard stories of them, vague whispers of creatures that lurk in the darkest corners of the world, bound to the curse that haunts Kieran's every step. But she's never imagined them to be real—until now.

Elara: (Shocked) Beasts? What do you mean? Are they—?

Kieran cuts her off with a sharp gesture, his eyes narrowing as he steps forward, leading her through the underbrush with swift, silent movements. The air around them seems to thrum with energy, the tension thick and almost tangible. Something is out there. Watching.

Kieran: (Urgently) Don't speak. Don't make a sound.

They move quickly, their pace quickening as they reach a small clearing in the woods. The moonlight floods the space, revealing the shadows of the trees stretching long and distorted across the ground. Elara can feel it—the heavy weight of something wrong, something unnatural that lingers in the air.

The Rising Darkness

Kieran stops suddenly, his hand gripping Elara's arm with surprising strength. His eyes are wide, filled with a terror she's never seen before. He's not looking at her—he's staring into the darkness that stretches beyond the clearing, where the trees are thick and black, hiding whatever lies beyond.

Kieran: (Whispering, hoarse) We're not alone.

Before Elara can respond, the air around them seems to crackle with an eerie, unnatural energy. Then, from the darkness, they hear it—footsteps, slow and deliberate, dragging across the ground like the weight of a thousand secrets. The trees sway, the shadows bending unnaturally as the creatures step into the moonlight.

Elara gasps, her blood running cold. The creatures that emerge from the shadows are unlike anything she's ever seen—tall, hunched figures, their eyes glowing with an otherworldly light. Their bodies are twisted, their limbs long and contorted, their movements predatory and unnatural. They are neither human nor animal, but something far worse—beasts forged from darkness itself.

Kieran: (Barely audible, in disbelief) The pack... they're here.

The creatures step closer, their eyes locked on Kieran as though they've been waiting for him. Elara can feel the malevolent intent in the air, the weight of death hanging over them like a cloud. Her breath catches in her throat as the first of the beasts steps forward, its claws scraping against the ground with a sound that sends shivers down her spine.

The Crying Wolf and the Darkest Night

Beast Leader: (Growling, low) The bloodline ends tonight.

Kieran's body stiffens, his eyes flashing with a mix of fear and defiance. Elara can feel the chill in the air as the beasts close in, their eyes fixed on Kieran with an almost predatory hunger. She knows, deep down, that this is no ordinary fight—it's a fight for his very soul.

Kieran: (Fiercely) You won't take me. Not tonight. Not ever.

But the beasts are closing in, their growls rising in pitch as they circle around them, and Elara knows they are running out of time. This is it—the darkness that Kieran has been running from, the darkness that's always been just beyond the horizon, is here. And it's only a matter of time before it takes them all.

Ten

Betrayal in the Moonlight

Scene 1: The Circle of Shadows

The forest holds its breath. The beasts circle Kieran and Elara, their eyes glowing like molten fire in the moonlight. The tension is palpable, thick and heavy, as if the very air around them has been charged with an ancient and deadly power. The ground beneath their feet trembles slightly, as if echoing the growls of the creatures who have come to claim Kieran's soul. Elara's heart races in her chest, her breath coming in short, quick bursts. She can feel Kieran beside her, his body tense, every muscle coiled like a spring, ready to fight for his life.

Kieran: (Low, urgent) Elara, stay close. Don't move unless I tell you.

The Crying Wolf and the Darkest Night

Elara nods, her body stiff with fear, but her mind is sharp. The creatures that surround them are closing in, their movements swift, predatory. She's heard stories, whispers of monsters that walk the earth, twisted by curses older than time itself. But nothing could have prepared her for this—a pack of creatures born from darkness, hungry and relentless.

One of the beasts snarls, its claws scraping the earth as it lunges forward, its eyes locked on Kieran. Kieran immediately steps into a defensive stance, his body radiating an unnatural energy that she can feel even from where she stands. His hands tremble, but his resolve is unbroken. He's ready to fight.

Kieran: (Shouting) Get back!

With a burst of speed, Kieran charges at the closest creature, his fists striking with the force of a man possessed. The beast hisses as Kieran's punch lands, but it doesn't falter. Instead, it lets out a low, menacing growl, its mouth opening wide to reveal teeth sharper than steel.

The creatures begin to close in, moving with terrifying speed. Elara feels her pulse quicken as one of the beasts shifts closer to her, its eyes never leaving hers. She stands frozen for a heartbeat, panic threatening to overtake her. But then, something shifts in the air—a sudden chill, a presence that feels out of place.

From the shadows, another figure emerges. A man, cloaked in darkness, steps into the clearing. His eyes gleam with a cold, cruel light, and Elara's heart skips a beat as she realizes who it is.

Elara: (Shocked) You…

The man steps forward, his presence commanding the attention of the beasts. They immediately fall back, their snarls silenced, as if bowing to him in deference. Elara's stomach churns with dread. This is no ordinary man. This is the one who's been pulling the strings, the one who's been orchestrating the chaos that's threatened Kieran and the world around them.

Man: (Darkly) You've been running for so long, Kieran. But you cannot escape the inevitable. It's time to face the truth.

Kieran's eyes narrow, a mix of recognition and fury flashing across his face. He takes a step back, positioning himself protectively in front of Elara.

Kieran: (Gravelly) What do you want, Darius? You know I won't join you. I'll never be your puppet.

Darius smirks, his expression cold and devoid of any emotion. The air around him seems to thrum with an eerie power, a darkness that pulls at the very edges of the night.

Darius: (Mockingly) You misunderstand me, Kieran. I don't want you to join me. I want you to die.

Elara feels her blood run cold at his words. She steps forward, positioning herself beside Kieran, her gaze never leaving Darius.

Elara: (Defiantly) No. You won't get away with this. You won't win.

Darius's eyes flicker toward Elara, his lips curling into a sinister smile.

Darius: (Coldly) You think you can stop me? You think you can save him? You're just as foolish as he is.

Kieran's jaw clenches, his fists tightening at his sides. He's about to speak when, suddenly, a sound cuts through the tension—a low, rumbling growl. The beasts, who had fallen back at Darius's arrival, now step forward again, their eyes burning with hunger. Kieran takes a deep breath, his body tensing as he prepares for the worst.

Elara: (Shouting) Kieran, don't fight them! We need a plan!

Kieran looks at her, his eyes filled with the weight of everything they've been through. The moment stretches between them, heavy and thick with unspoken words. And then, as if in slow motion, Kieran turns to face the pack of beasts, his face set in grim determination.

Kieran: (Harshly) There's no plan. We fight.

Before Elara can react, Kieran lunges at the nearest creature, his movements swift and brutal. He fights with everything he has, but the beasts are relentless. They are faster, stronger, and more dangerous than anything he's faced before. Elara watches in horror as Kieran's strikes land on the beasts, but they barely seem to faze them. She can see the desperation in his eyes as he struggles to hold them off.

But then, a movement catches her eye—a flash of light, a figure moving through the shadows, almost too fast for her to catch. Her heart races as she realizes that someone else is here, someone who shouldn't be. Someone who's been watching them this entire time.

Elara: (Whispering) No... it can't be.

Kieran: (Shouting, between gritted teeth) Elara! Get back!

Before Elara can respond, the figure steps into the clearing. She freezes, her breath catching in her throat as the last person she expected to see stands before her. It's... it's him.

Elara: (Horrified) Roran? What... What are you doing here?

Roran stands there, his face a mask of cold indifference. He doesn't speak, but his eyes are filled with a darkness that makes Elara's blood run cold. She takes a step back, unsure of what to believe. She thought she knew him—she thought he was an ally. But now, as he stands before her, his posture rigid and tense, there's something off. Something wrong.

Kieran pauses in the midst of fighting, his eyes darting to Roran. His face hardens, his expression shifting from surprise to something darker, more knowing.

Kieran: (Snarling) You... You were part of this all along, weren't you?

Roran's lips curl into a small, almost imperceptible smile. He steps forward, his movements fluid, like a predator stalking its prey.

Roran: (Coolly) I was never your ally, Kieran. Not really. I've always had my own plans. And those plans never included saving you.

Elara's heart drops into her stomach. She takes a step back, her mind racing as the truth begins to unravel in front of her. Roran—her friend, her ally—has been playing them both from the beginning. He's been working with Darius, manipulating them, using their trust to further his own dark goals.

Elara: (In disbelief) No. You... you lied to me. You lied to both of us.

Roran's eyes glimmer with an unsettling coldness as he steps toward her, his gaze never leaving her face.

Roran: (Slightly mocking) I didn't lie. I simply didn't tell you everything. You were never meant to know the truth, Elara. You were a tool. A pawn in this game. Just like Kieran.

Kieran's eyes flare with fury, his hands shaking as he turns to face Roran fully. His voice is filled with a rage that matches the burning intensity in his eyes.

Kieran: (Furiously) You used her. You used us both!

Betrayal in the Moonlight

Roran's expression remains impassive, as if Kieran's anger means nothing to him.

Roran: (Coldly) I'm not here to explain myself. I'm here to finish what I started. The pack, Darius, all of it—it's part of a plan. And you, Kieran, were always meant to fall. You just didn't know it yet.

The beasts begin to move, stepping forward as though they're waiting for Roran's signal. Elara's pulse spikes, her mind racing. She can't believe it. Everything she thought she knew, everything she thought she could trust, has been a lie.

Elara: (Shouting) Kieran! We need to get out of here—now!

Kieran's face is full of fury, but beneath it, there's a profound sadness. He knows they're trapped. He knows that Roran's betrayal is the final blow in this long, dark journey. The beasts close in, their hunger palpable, and Elara feels the weight of the situation settle heavily around her.

Kieran: (Quietly, with resignation) It's too late.

The full moon above them seems to dim for a moment, as if mourning the darkness that's closing in. The pack moves in, and in that moment, Kieran and Elara know that they are about to face the ultimate betrayal—one that will forever change the course of their fate.

Eleven

The Broken Sea

Scene 1: The Tides of Betrayal

The moon hangs high, a pale shard in the sky, casting its light onto the jagged coastline. The sea below is restless, waves crashing against the rocks with a ferocity that matches the turmoil within Kieran's heart. His eyes are hard, narrowed against the wind, his posture taut with fury and betrayal. He stands at the edge of the cliff, staring down at the churning waters below, the roar of the ocean filling his ears. Elara is a few steps behind him, her breath shallow, her mind racing as she struggles to make sense of everything that has just transpired.

Elara: (Shakily) Kieran… we have to get out of here. Roran's betrayal—it's too much. We can't stay here.

Kieran doesn't answer immediately. His eyes remain fixed

The Broken Sea

on the horizon, where the darkness of the sea and sky blend into an indistinguishable blackness. The wind whips through his hair, but he stands motionless, as if frozen in place by the gravity of the moment.

Elara: (Urgently) Kieran, please... I can't do this without you. We need to leave. We need to find a way to stop this—before it's too late.

Kieran turns slowly, his expression unreadable. His gaze locks with hers, and for a moment, it's as though the world falls away. All the chaos, the lies, the beasts, and even the curse—none of it matters. Just her. The woman who has stood beside him through it all.

Kieran: (Roughly) I don't know how much longer I can keep running, Elara. Everywhere I go, there's darkness. It's following me, hunting me. And now... Roran... he's a part of it. I can't escape it.

Elara's heart twists at his words, her breath catching in her throat. She takes a step closer, closing the distance between them. Her voice is soft, filled with an unspoken plea.

Elara: (Gently) You don't have to face this alone. I'm with you. We'll figure it out together. But you can't give up. Not now. Not after everything.

Kieran's gaze softens, just for a moment, but then it hardens again, the weight of his curse and the burden of betrayal settling like a stone in his chest.

The Crying Wolf and the Darkest Night

Kieran: (Murmuring) The curse isn't something I can fight. It's part of me. It's inside me. I've tried to ignore it, to run from it. But it always catches up. And Roran… he's always been part of the plan. He's been using me. And worse—he's been using you.

Elara recoils slightly at the mention of Roran's manipulation, but she doesn't back down. She reaches out, her fingers brushing his arm, her touch warm against the cold air.

Elara: (Softly) I don't care what he's done, Kieran. I care about you. You are not the curse. You are not the monster. And we will find a way to stop it. Together.

Kieran closes his eyes, his jaw clenching, as if trying to hold back the flood of emotions threatening to break through. He turns his head toward the sea again, his fists tightening at his sides.

Kieran: (Harshly) I'm not sure I even believe that anymore. But… I'll fight. For you. For us.

The moment lingers in the air between them, but it's interrupted by the sudden sound of a distant crash—louder than the rest of the waves. Kieran's head snaps up, his senses immediately alert, and Elara's hand tightens on his arm. Something is wrong.

Elara: (Whispering) What was that?

Kieran: (Low) Stay close. We're not alone.

The Broken Sea

As if on cue, a shadow moves in the distance—on the far side of the cliff, near the narrow path that leads down toward the shore. Kieran's eyes narrow, his muscles tensing. The shadow moves again, closer now, too fast to be human. Elara feels the hairs on the back of her neck rise, a chill running through her body.

Elara: (Tensely) Kieran… what is it?

Kieran doesn't answer. Instead, he steps forward, his hand gripping Elara's wrist firmly, pulling her along with him. The path toward the shore is narrow, treacherous, and the cliffside drops sharply beneath them, the sea roaring violently below. The shadow grows larger with every passing second, and then, from the corner of her eye, Elara sees it—something moving swiftly, climbing the rocks with unnatural grace.

Elara: (Horrified) No… it can't be…

Kieran's voice is a low growl, filled with a primal fear that Elara has never heard from him before.

Kieran: (Urgently) It's them. The pack. They've found us. We need to move—now!

They break into a sprint, moving as quickly as they can down the path toward the shore. The wind howls around them, and the sea crashes angrily against the rocks below. But even as they run, Elara feels the press of the beasts closing in on them, their presence growing stronger with each passing second.

The Crying Wolf and the Darkest Night

As they reach the bottom of the cliff, the shore opens up before them—a jagged, rocky beach stretching out toward the horizon. But there's no safety to be found here. The creatures are everywhere now, their eyes glowing with hunger and rage. Elara can feel their eyes on her, watching, waiting for the right moment to strike.

Kieran stops suddenly, pulling Elara to a halt with a tight grip on her arm. He's looking at the far end of the beach, where something is moving—something that shouldn't be there.

Kieran: (Whispering, tense) There's something else. We're not just running from the pack anymore. There's something worse... something I didn't expect.

Elara follows his gaze, her heart pounding in her chest. A figure steps from the shadows, tall and imposing. It's a man—a familiar man. Her stomach drops as she recognizes him. The face is unmistakable. It's Roran.

Elara: (Shocked) No... Roran...

Kieran's fists clench at his sides, his eyes filled with a mixture of disbelief and fury. He steps forward, positioning himself between Elara and Roran, his body a shield.

Kieran: (Angrily) What do you want now, Roran?

Roran's expression is cold, detached, as though the bond they once shared has meant nothing to him. He steps closer, his eyes never leaving Kieran's face.

The Broken Sea

Roran: (Mockingly) You really thought you could outrun the curse, Kieran? You really thought you could stop it? You're a fool.

Elara feels the weight of his words sink in, but it's not the betrayal that cuts the deepest—it's the finality in Roran's voice. As if this was always meant to be. Kieran's fight, her own struggle, has always been part of a plan they never understood.

Elara: (Shakily) You— You were the one who did this. You were the one who set everything in motion.

Roran turns his gaze to her, his lips curling into a smile that doesn't reach his eyes.

Roran: (Coldly) Did you really think I would help you? Did you really think you could change the fate that's been written in your blood? You're as much a part of this as Kieran. And you always have been.

Kieran's voice cracks as he steps forward, his hands shaking with barely contained rage.

Kieran: (Fiercely) You used us. You manipulated us, every step of the way. All for what? To break me? To break her?

Roran smiles, his eyes gleaming with a twisted satisfaction.

Roran: (Darkly) You don't understand, Kieran. You never did. The darkness... it's coming for you. For both of you. And there's no escape this time.

Before Kieran can respond, the ground beneath their feet trembles again. Elara looks up in horror as she sees the pack of beasts closing in on them, their eyes glowing with hunger. But this time, something is different. The air is charged with an ancient, foreboding energy. The beasts are no longer simply predators—they are instruments of something far darker.

Kieran turns to Elara, his face set with a grim determination.

Kieran: (Harshly) Run, Elara. Now!

Elara doesn't hesitate. She turns and runs, her heart pounding in her chest, but she can't escape the feeling that something far worse is coming for them. The beasts are upon them, but they're not the ones Elara fears now. It's the man who stands behind them, smiling as if this is all part of a game.

Kieran: (Yelling) Elara, don't stop!

The broken sea crashes against the shore, but even the sound of the waves is drowned out by the thundering steps of the beasts and the shadow of the man who has betrayed them both.

Twelve

A Forbidden Kiss

~~~~~

Scene 1: The Edge of the Abyss

The wind howls through the jagged cliffs, its voice a harsh cry that echoes through the desolate night. Kieran and Elara stand at the precipice of a crumbling stone tower, high above the darkened sea. Below them, the waves crash violently against the rocks, the relentless pull of the ocean mirroring the turmoil in Kieran's chest. The moon hangs heavy in the sky, its light casting eerie shadows on the ruins around them. The air is thick with tension, an unspoken force drawing them together, yet the distance between them has never felt greater.

Kieran: (Gravelly, staring out at the horizon) We've run so far, Elara. We've fought so hard, but I'm not sure there's any place left to hide from this curse.

The Crying Wolf and the Darkest Night

Elara stands behind him, her heart heavy with a thousand unsaid words. Her chest tightens with the weight of Kieran's pain, the burden he carries. She's seen him fight—fought beside him—but she's never seen him like this, broken, shattered in a way that makes her own heart ache. She steps forward, her voice barely above a whisper.

Elara: (Softly) You don't have to fight alone, Kieran. Not anymore. Whatever happens, we'll face it together.

Kieran turns slowly, his face shadowed, but his eyes searching hers, as if trying to decipher the truth in her words. His jaw clenches, a flicker of doubt passing across his face. He's always been alone in this fight. The curse, the creatures, the darkness—it has always been a battle within him. And now, standing here with Elara, a woman who has come to mean more than he can admit, he's terrified of what will happen to her when everything finally falls apart.

Kieran: (Hoarsely) I don't want to pull you into this, Elara. I never did. You're not supposed to be here. This curse... this life... it's not meant for you. You don't deserve it.

Elara's breath catches in her throat at his words, her heart aching as if it were breaking in two. She takes a step closer, her hand reaching out to him, but he steps back, his gaze falling to the ground. The air between them is thick with unspoken emotions, with feelings that neither of them is ready to confront.

Elara: (Shakily) Don't say that. Don't push me away, Kieran.

A Forbidden Kiss

You're not the only one who's been fighting. I've been with you from the start. I've seen what you've done, what you've sacrificed. And I'm not going anywhere.

Kieran's gaze snaps up to hers, his expression filled with a mixture of frustration and vulnerability.

Kieran: (Urgently) You don't understand. I'm not the man you think I am. I'm not the person you think I can be. I've done terrible things, Elara. Things I can never undo.

Elara feels her heart twist in her chest as she steps forward, her voice trembling with a fierce urgency.

Elara: (Softly) I know you. I know the person you are, Kieran. I see the good in you. No matter what you've done or what's been done to you, that's not who you are. You are not defined by your past, by the curse. You're so much more than that.

The words hang in the air between them, the weight of them sinking deep into Kieran's soul. For the first time, he feels the walls he's built around himself begin to crumble. The words she speaks—her unwavering faith in him—pierce through the darkness that has consumed him for so long. He's always believed that he was a monster, a creature bound by the curse. But standing here, with Elara's hand outstretched, he begins to question that belief.

Kieran: (Voice breaking) I don't know if I can be the man you want me to be, Elara. I don't know if I even deserve your love.

The Crying Wolf and the Darkest Night

Elara's hand gently cups his face, her touch warm against the coldness of his skin. Her thumb traces the lines of his jaw, and for a moment, the world around them seems to disappear. It's just the two of them—standing on the edge of the abyss, facing their fears, their pasts, and the undeniable bond that has grown between them.

Elara: (Firmly) You don't have to be perfect, Kieran. You don't have to be anyone else. You are enough. You've always been enough.

Kieran's heart pounds in his chest, his breath coming in shallow gasps. He wants to believe her, wants to give in to the feelings that have been building between them, but the fear holds him back. The fear of what he is, of what he's capable of, and the fear of losing her in the process.

But in the depths of his heart, something shifts. A yearning, a longing he can no longer ignore. He knows that he's been running from the truth for too long—that the darkness he's carried within him is not the only thing that defines him. That love, too, has a place in his heart.

Kieran: (Whispering) I don't deserve you... but I can't stay away from you.

Elara's eyes glisten with unshed tears, her lips trembling as she moves closer to him. The distance between them feels unbearable, as though the very air crackles with the intensity of what is about to happen. She reaches up, her fingers brushing his lips softly, and in that moment, Kieran's breath hitches in

A Forbidden Kiss

his throat.

Elara: (Softly) You don't have to deserve it, Kieran. You just have to let me in.

There's a hesitation in his eyes, a flicker of fear that passes through him like a shadow, but then he lowers his head, his forehead resting gently against hers. The world seems to stand still as their breath mingles in the night air, and for a fleeting moment, nothing else matters.

Then, without warning, Kieran closes the gap between them, his lips crashing into hers with a fierce desperation. The kiss is raw, filled with all the emotions they've both been holding back—pain, longing, fear, and a desperate need for connection. Elara's hands tangle in his hair, pulling him closer, her body pressed against his as if she could feel the darkness that still lingers inside him. But in that moment, the curse, the monsters, the betrayal—all of it fades away. There's only the two of them, lost in the heat of their kiss.

Kieran: (Breathing heavily, pulling away) Elara…

Elara's eyes are closed, her lips swollen from the intensity of the kiss. She breathes out a soft laugh, her voice low and intimate.

Elara: (Whispering) What are we doing, Kieran? We shouldn't be doing this. It's too dangerous.

Kieran stares down at her, his hands trembling as they rest on her shoulders. His gaze is filled with a mixture of longing and regret, but there's something else there too—a flicker of hope. A hope he hasn't allowed himself to feel in a long time.

Kieran: (Quietly) I know. But I can't help it. I can't help how I feel about you.

Elara's breath catches in her throat at his words. She can see it now—the conflict within him, the battle between the curse and the man he wants to be. She knows the danger they're both in. She knows that their love is forbidden, that the darkness will try to tear them apart. But in this moment, it doesn't matter. She can't turn away from him, no matter the cost.

Elara: (Softly, determined) Then don't. Don't turn away from me. Not now. Not when we're so close to everything we've been fighting for.

For a moment, they stand there in the quiet of the night, the sound of the crashing waves and the distant howls of the beasts serving as a backdrop to the storm that rages within them both. And then, with a final, soft kiss, they both know—this moment, this love, is a fleeting thing. A forbidden kiss, sealed with the promise of what could be, and the uncertainty of what the future holds.

But as the moonlight bathes them both in its cold, unyielding glow, Kieran and Elara know one thing for certain—their hearts are bound together, and no curse, no betrayal, can ever change that.

Thirteen

The Hunt Begins

Scene 1: The Shadows Stir

The night is thick with silence, a quiet that feels unnatural in its heaviness. Kieran and Elara stand at the edge of the forest, their backs to the ruins of the old tower, where the moonlight filters through the sparse trees like silver threads weaving their fate. The hunt has begun.

Elara stands a few paces behind Kieran, her heart racing in her chest. The kiss, the fleeting moment of warmth and tenderness, now feels like a distant memory, replaced by the dark, palpable sense of danger that presses in from all sides. Kieran is tense, his body coiled like a spring, eyes scanning the shadows for any sign of movement.

Kieran: (Low and tense) They're coming. I can feel it.

Elara moves closer, her voice steady despite the fear creeping into her chest.

Elara: (Softly) We have to get ahead of them, Kieran. If we stay here, we'll be trapped.

Kieran: (Harshly) I can't run anymore, Elara. Not from them. Not from what I am.

Elara's gaze softens as she steps closer to him, her hand reaching out to gently touch his arm. His muscles are tight under her fingertips, his skin cool to the touch, and for a moment, she wonders if she can still reach him—if she can still pull him back from the abyss he's so determined to dive into.

Elara: (Quietly) You don't have to do this alone. I'm with you. I won't let them take you.

Kieran looks at her, the intensity in his eyes flickering with something like doubt. His jaw clenches as he turns away from her, his fists tightening at his sides. The air around them is thick with the scent of the forest, the distant sound of a howling wind, but underneath it all, there's something more—something darker.

Kieran: (Low) They won't stop until they have me, Elara. I've spent my entire life running from the curse, hiding from what I am. But tonight, the hunt begins. And I won't be able to outrun it this time.

Elara takes a step forward, her eyes steady, locking onto his.

The Hunt Begins

Elara: (Firmly) Then we fight. Together.

Kieran's gaze flickers to her, a flicker of something deep in his eyes—a mixture of fear and yearning. He's seen the darkness, the monsters that stalk him, the beast that lives within him, but there's something in her that makes him question everything he's known. He's never had anyone like her, not in his entire life. She's not afraid of him, even though she should be. But in this moment, all he can feel is the cold certainty of what's to come.

Kieran: (Shaking his head) You don't understand. This isn't just about me. The pack will come for you too. They'll tear through everything, destroy anyone who gets in their way. I can't protect you, Elara. Not from this.

Elara reaches out, her hand finding his, her grip tight and unyielding.

Elara: (With quiet resolve) You won't have to protect me alone. We protect each other. We fight together.

Kieran's breath hitches as he stares at her hand, at the way she holds him, steady and unwavering. For a moment, the world feels distant, and the only thing that matters is her. He knows she's right. They've come too far, fought too hard to turn back now. He can't lose her—not now, not when they're so close to uncovering the truth. Not when they're so close to breaking the curse.

Kieran: (Softly) You're crazy, you know that?

Elara smiles softly, a glimmer of determination in her eyes.

Elara: (With a smirk) Crazy enough to believe we can win.

Kieran looks at her for a long moment, his eyes searching hers, and then he exhales a sharp breath, his resolve hardening. The hunt is coming. He can feel it in the air, the tension growing with every passing second. The wind stirs once more, and in that gust, he hears it—the sound of a distant howl. The pack is close.

Kieran: (Urgently) We need to move. Now.

Without another word, he pulls Elara along, his steps swift and purposeful as they disappear deeper into the forest, their footsteps muffled by the thick underbrush. The moonlight cuts through the trees, casting long shadows on the ground, but Kieran moves with a predator's grace, his senses sharp, tuned to the sounds around them. Elara follows closely behind, her breath quick and shallow, her heart hammering in her chest.

The hunt has begun.

Scene 2: The Chase Begins

Hours pass in the dark, the forest seeming to close in around them as they move deeper into its heart. The trees grow taller here, their twisted branches reaching toward the sky like gnarled fingers. The air is thick with the scent of damp earth and pine, but there's something else too—a faint trace of decay, as if the forest itself is hiding a dark secret.

The Hunt Begins

Elara feels it before she hears it—a presence, something moving just beyond the trees. She stops, her breath caught in her throat as she scans the shadows. She sees nothing, but the feeling is unmistakable—something is watching them.

Elara: (Whispering, tense) Kieran… they're here.

Kieran stops beside her, his muscles coiled, his eyes darting around them. He's no longer the man he was—there's a coldness to him now, a primal awareness that pulses through him. He can feel their presence too, the pack drawing closer, closing in like wolves circling their prey.

Kieran: (Low) Don't move. Don't make a sound.

They stand still, the only sound the wind rustling through the trees. Elara holds her breath, her senses on high alert. Then, in the distance, she hears it—a low growl, the unmistakable sound of something large and dangerous moving through the underbrush.

Elara's heart skips a beat, her eyes wide with fear.

Elara: (Shaking) They're coming.

Kieran grips her arm tightly, pulling her toward him as he crouches low to the ground, his eyes scanning the darkness. He's no longer Kieran, the man she's come to care for. He's the beast—the predator, the hunter, and he's preparing for what's to come.

Kieran: (Urgently) We have to keep moving. We can't let them surround us. Stay close to me.

Elara nods, her eyes locked on his as she takes a deep breath and steels herself. She's not afraid of him—she's not afraid of the monsters he's been running from. But she's afraid of losing him. Of losing everything.

As they move forward, the forest seems to close in around them, the trees pressing in tighter, the ground uneven and treacherous beneath their feet. The growls grow louder now, closer, as if the pack is circling them, waiting for the right moment to strike.

And then, just as they round a bend in the path, it happens. A figure emerges from the shadows—a tall, hulking form with glowing eyes. Kieran doesn't hesitate. He's already in motion, his body moving with a speed and precision that only a creature like him can possess. The figure lunges toward them, but Kieran is faster, his claws slashing through the air, catching the beast across the chest with a brutal force.

The creature howls in pain, stumbling back, and Kieran presses forward, his eyes wild with fury.

Kieran: (Roaring) You want me? Come and get me!

Elara gasps as she watches the creature recover, its snarling mouth wide open, teeth bared, and the air around them crackles with the power of the hunt. Another creature emerges from the trees, followed by a third, and Elara realizes with a jolt that

The Hunt Begins

they are surrounded.

Elara: (Panicked) Kieran! There's too many of them!

Kieran: (Grimly) Don't stop. Keep running.

With a final, desperate glance toward Elara, Kieran spins, his claws ripping into the beast that dares to approach them. The forest is alive with the sounds of battle, of snarls and growls, the fierce clashes of predator and prey. But even as the pack closes in, even as the darkness threatens to swallow them whole, Kieran fights with the ferocity of a creature desperate to survive.

And Elara, by his side, feels the weight of the curse, the hunt, and the love they both refuse to deny.

Fourteen

The Heart of the Wolf

Scene 1: The Forbidden Path

The moon looms overhead, its pale light casting long, eerie shadows across the ancient forest. The wind has died down, leaving an unsettling silence that hangs in the air, thick with tension. The ground beneath Kieran's feet is soft and treacherous, thick with moss and tangled roots that seem to reach up like the fingers of ghosts. Every step is calculated, every sound amplified in the stillness of the night.

Kieran and Elara move silently, their breath shallow, their senses heightened. Kieran's eyes flicker constantly to the shadows, his body stiff and poised for action. He can feel them—feel the pack drawing closer, the hunt still not finished. His heart beats erratically in his chest, the pull of the curse gnawing at him, the beast within him tugging with a force he's barely able to control. He should have let Elara go. He should have sent her away, but the words never came. He couldn't let her leave. Not after everything they've shared.

Elara, walking beside him, is every bit as tense as he is. Her hand brushes against his in a brief, fleeting connection, a reminder of the bond they share, and yet even that feels fragile now. The hunt has taken everything from them—everything except the will to survive. And the love they refuse to abandon.

Elara: (Voice low, breathless) Kieran, where are we going? This doesn't look like the path we were following before.

Kieran's gaze flickers to her, his expression shadowed with uncertainty, but there's something else there too—a determination that burns deeper than the doubt.

Kieran: (Grimly) We're not running anymore. It's time to end this.

Elara feels her chest tighten at his words, her heart pounding as she watches him. There's a darkness in his eyes now—one that's deeper than any curse she's encountered. This isn't just about surviving anymore. This is something more. Something that might cost them everything.

Elara: (Urgently) What are you talking about? Kieran, you can't face them alone. This isn't something you can fight on your own.

Kieran: (Sharp) I'm not facing them alone. I'm facing myself.

Elara's breath catches in her throat. The weight of his words lingers in the space between them like a physical force. She knows what he means. She's seen the beast inside him, the monster that howls at the moon, the creature that's torn him apart for years. And in this moment, she realizes that the real battle isn't against the pack. It's against the very thing that Kieran is—against the darkness that lives within him.

Elara steps closer, her hand reaching for his again. This time, he doesn't pull away. Their fingers intertwine, the contact small but grounding in the storm that rages around them.

Elara: (Softly) I won't let you fight alone. We'll face it together, Kieran. Whatever it is, whatever this… this thing is inside you, we can find a way to destroy it. Together.

Kieran looks at her, his eyes filled with a storm of conflicting emotions. He wants to believe her, wants to believe that there's a way out of this nightmare. But the fear that claws at him, that tightens in his chest, is too strong. He doesn't know if he can escape the beast inside him. He doesn't know if he can control it. And worse—he's afraid that, in the end, it might consume him completely.

Kieran: (Voice barely above a whisper) You don't understand, Elara. The curse isn't something I can just fight off. It's not that simple. The heart of the wolf—it's not just a curse. It's who I am.

Elara feels her heart sink at his words, but she stands firm. She can see the battle within him, the struggle between the man she loves and the beast that haunts him. And she knows, deep down, that the only way to win this fight is to confront it head-on. To face whatever this darkness is, together.

Elara: (Stepping forward, voice resolute) Then we'll face it. We'll face the heart of the wolf and break it. I believe in you, Kieran.

For a long moment, they stand there, the forest holding its breath around them, before Kieran finally nods. The air between them crackles with a fierce, quiet intensity. The pack might be coming, but the real enemy lies within. And they have no choice but to move forward.

Scene 2: The Heart of the Wolf

The deeper they move into the forest, the more the world around them begins to shift. The trees become thicker, their bark twisted and gnarled, the shadows darker, as if the very earth itself is closing in. The sense of unease grows stronger, the air charged with a palpable energy that seems to thrum beneath their feet.

Kieran's steps quicken as the sensation grows. He can feel the pull—the call of the curse beckoning him forward. It's close. Too close. The power that lurks inside him is stirring, waking, demanding to be free. He can feel it, feel the wolf inside him pushing against the surface, clawing to be released. His breath comes in shallow gasps as the pressure builds in his chest.

Kieran: (Voice strained) We're almost there…

Elara looks around, her senses on high alert. The forest seems to watch them, the trees groaning and creaking as though alive. The air is thick with the smell of earth, of decay—and something else. Something far darker.

Elara: (Whispering) Kieran… what is this place?

Kieran doesn't answer right away. His focus is entirely on the path ahead of them. They're close now—so close. The heart of the wolf. The source of his curse. The place where everything began. And he can feel it. He can feel it thrumming in his veins, calling to him like an insatiable hunger.

Suddenly, a figure emerges from the shadows, tall and imposing, its eyes glowing with an unnatural, predatory light. The wolf-like creature steps into their path, blocking their way. It's more than just a beast. It's something ancient, something older than the curse itself.

Creature: (Deep, rumbling voice) You have come for the heart. But you are not prepared, Kieran. No one ever is.

Kieran stops in his tracks, his eyes narrowing as the creature's voice washes over him. This isn't just another one of the pack. This is something else. Something older. A guardian of sorts. His instincts flare—he knows this creature, knows it's been waiting for him all his life.

Kieran: (Low, guttural) I've been waiting for this. Waiting to end it.

The Heart of the Wolf

The creature's eyes flicker to Elara, its gaze calculating, as if deciding whether or not she's worth acknowledging. Then it looks back at Kieran, its lips curling into a snarl.

Creature: (Mocking) You think you can end the curse? You think you can destroy what was forged in the very heart of the wolf? It's in your blood, Kieran. You will never escape it.

Elara steps forward, her voice firm, cutting through the tension.

Elara: (Defiant) We will escape it. We will break it. Kieran's not a monster. He's a man. And no curse, no matter how old or strong, can change that.

Kieran's heart lurches at her words, but the creature merely laughs, a low, chilling sound that seems to echo from all around them.

Creature: (Amused) A man? Kieran, you are no mere man. The blood of wolves runs through you. It runs through your veins. The curse isn't just a part of you. It is you.

Kieran's gaze hardens as he takes a step forward, his fists clenching at his sides.

Kieran: (Angrily) No! I am not the curse. I will not be what you want me to be.

The creature's eyes flash with malicious delight.

Creature: (Coldly) Then come. Prove it. But know this—once

you face the heart of the wolf, you will never be the same.

And with those words, the creature vanishes back into the shadows, its presence lingering like a dark omen. Kieran turns to Elara, his expression conflicted, but there's a fire in his eyes—a defiance that wasn't there before.

Kieran: (Determined) We're almost there. It's time to face the heart of the wolf. It's time to break this curse… once and for all.

Fifteen

The Rising Moon

Scene 1: The Edge of Darkness

The forest is silent now, the sounds of the hunt fading into the night like echoes of a dream. The path ahead is dark, swallowed by the towering trees, their twisted branches reaching out like gnarled hands, beckoning them closer. The air is thick with the scent of moss and damp earth, the smell of the forest's ancient heart. Kieran and Elara walk side by side, their footsteps muffled by the forest floor, but the tension between them is palpable, a heavy weight that neither of them can shake.

Elara glances at Kieran, her gaze lingering on his tense form. His jaw is clenched, his hands balled into fists at his sides, and the deep, restless energy within him feels like an earthquake waiting to tear through the ground beneath their feet. She knows he's struggling. She can see it in the way his eyes dart back and forth, always searching the shadows. He's fighting with something inside him—a hunger, a need—that she can feel even without understanding it completely. And the worst part? He's not even sure if he can control it anymore.

Elara: (Softly) Kieran, talk to me. What's going on inside your head?

Kieran's eyes flick to her, and for a brief moment, he almost looks like the man she met all those weeks ago—the man who showed her kindness, the man who, despite everything, wanted to believe in something better. But that moment quickly fades, replaced by the fierce intensity of the wolf inside him. His lips curl into a faint smile, one that's more bitter than reassuring.

Kieran: (Grimly) There's nothing left to talk about, Elara. The heart of the wolf is more than just a curse. It's a part of me. It's always been there, and I've been running from it my whole life. But tonight... tonight, I can't run anymore.

The words hit her like a blow, and Elara feels the sting of fear tighten her chest. She's not afraid of him—not the Kieran she knows, not the man who would fight for her—but she's afraid of what he's becoming. And she's terrified of the darkness that's pulling him further and further away from her.

Elara: (Urgently) You don't have to face this alone, Kieran. We can do this together. I—

Kieran cuts her off, his voice low and strained, barely audible over the wind that starts to pick up. His breath comes in quick, shallow gasps as he looks up, his eyes locked on the rising moon above them.

Kieran: (Hoarse) The moon... it's rising faster than it should. It's almost as if something is pulling it—something stronger than I've ever felt before.

Elara follows his gaze, her heart racing as she looks at the full moon, its pale light cutting through the trees, casting an eerie glow over everything. The moon seems to pulse, almost alive, its light flickering like the heartbeat of something ancient. The feeling in the air shifts, and Elara feels the weight of it in her chest, the deep unease crawling up her spine like a cold hand. She shudders but holds her ground.

Elara: (Quietly) What does it mean? What's happening?

Kieran's expression darkens as he slowly turns away from the moon, his face tightening in frustration and fear. The transformation is beginning. The blood of the wolf is stirring inside him, urging him to embrace the change, to give in to the animal within him. And yet, despite everything, Kieran holds on—clinging to the last thread of his humanity, fighting a battle that feels like it will consume him whole.

Kieran: (Grimly) It means the curse is reaching its peak. The rising moon is a signal—one that's been building for years. It's calling me, Elara. Calling me to the heart of the wolf, to the place where it all began.

The Crying Wolf and the Darkest Night

Elara takes a step toward him, her voice desperate now, filled with the urgency of someone who knows that time is running out.

Elara: (Pleading) Kieran, please. You don't have to go there. We can stop this. Together, we can stop it.

Kieran turns to face her, his eyes flashing with a mixture of pain and determination. The wolf's power thrums beneath his skin, and for a moment, he looks like a stranger. The man she loves is still there, buried deep inside, but the wolf is taking over, and Elara doesn't know how much longer she can hold onto him.

Kieran: (Coldly) You don't understand. I've spent my life running from this, hiding from what I am. But there's no escaping it now. The heart of the wolf is the only place where I can end it. Where I can destroy the curse for good.

He turns away from her, walking toward the darkened path that leads deeper into the forest, the shadows growing thicker with each step. Elara stands frozen for a moment, her heart aching as she watches him, torn between the fear of losing him and the need to save him. She knows he's right—this battle isn't something they can run from. It's something they have to face. But the thought of him walking into the darkness alone is unbearable.

Elara: (Shouting) Kieran! Wait!

Kieran doesn't stop. His pace quickens, his body moving with

The Rising Moon

the inhuman speed of the wolf. Elara's heart races as she hurries after him, her breath ragged in the cold air. She won't lose him. Not now. Not when they're so close to the truth.

Scene 2: The Heart of the Wolf

The path ahead is dark, almost suffocating, and the air feels charged, as if the world itself is holding its breath. The closer they get to the heart of the wolf, the more Elara feels the change. The trees seem to bend toward them, the ground slick with something otherworldly. The moon above them burns with an intensity she's never seen before, casting shadows that twist and writhe in the night.

Kieran's eyes flash with an animal intensity as he strides forward, his senses on high alert. He can feel the wolf inside him, pushing against the walls he's tried to build. It's stronger now, demanding release, but Kieran refuses to give in. Not yet. He's determined to find a way to break the curse—once and for all.

But as they reach the clearing where the heart of the wolf is said to reside, Kieran stops. The air grows thick with power, and the ground trembles beneath their feet. In the center of the clearing stands a massive stone altar, its surface etched with ancient runes that glow faintly in the moonlight. Around it, the trees seem to bow, their branches tangled like a web, as if trying to keep them from approaching.

Elara stops beside him, her eyes wide with awe and fear as she looks at the altar.

The Crying Wolf and the Darkest Night

Elara: (Breathless) This is it... isn't it? This is where it all began.

Kieran's voice is low, almost reverent, as he steps forward, his eyes fixed on the altar.

Kieran: (Softly) This is where the curse was born. The heart of the wolf. And now... now it's time to end it.

The ground beneath them shakes again, more violently this time. The trees creak and groan, their twisted limbs reaching for them like grasping hands. Elara's heart pounds in her chest as she watches Kieran, the transformation starting to take hold of him. His breathing becomes labored, his muscles trembling as the wolf claws at him from within. But still, he stands firm, his eyes never leaving the altar.

Elara: (Quietly, with resolve) Kieran, you don't have to do this alone. I'm right here. Whatever happens next... we do it together.

Kieran's eyes flicker to her, his expression hardening, but there's something softer in his gaze—something that makes her believe that, despite the odds, despite everything, he hasn't given up on them.

Kieran: (Grimly) We don't have a choice, Elara. This is the only way.

And with that, Kieran steps forward, placing his hands on the stone altar. The moonlight above them flares, and the runes on the altar begin to glow brighter, casting a cold light over the clearing. Elara watches in horror as Kieran's body shudders, the change beginning in earnest. His eyes bleed from human to wolf, his skin rippling with the force of the transformation. And as the full moon rises higher in the sky, the curse reaches its peak.

Kieran: (Grunting, his voice shifting) Elara... it's... it's too late.

But Elara steps forward, her heart beating with determination.

Elara: (Firmly) It's never too late, Kieran. I won't let you go. Not now. Not ever.

And together, as the wolf howls beneath the rising moon, they prepare to face whatever comes next.

Sixteen

The Breaking Point

Scene 1: The Howl of the Wolf

The moon hangs high in the sky, its light a sickly, cold glow that casts an eerie sheen across the clearing. The air vibrates with power, charged and restless, as though the very earth beneath their feet knows what's coming. Kieran stands at the altar, his hands gripping the stone as his body contorts and trembles with the force of the transformation. The wolf inside him claws at the surface, its hunger raw, its need primal. His bones crack and snap, his flesh stretching and twisting into something inhuman. His mouth opens in a scream, but only the howl of the wolf emerges—a sound so mournful and full of pain that it echoes through the night, shattering the silence around them.

Elara steps forward, her heart racing, her breath caught in her

The Breaking Point

throat. She watches as Kieran fights against the change, his body locked in an agonizing battle, his eyes flickering between human and beast. The wolf inside him is close to the surface now, but there's something else too—a deep, aching sorrow that radiates from him like a wave. Elara can feel it, feel his pain and confusion like a physical weight pressing against her chest. She knows this is the moment, the breaking point. Kieran is teetering on the edge, and if she doesn't act now, he might fall into the abyss.

Elara: (Urgently, stepping forward) Kieran, listen to me! You don't have to fight it alone. We can do this! We can stop the curse!

Kieran's head snaps toward her, his eyes wild with fear and confusion. His breathing is ragged, his chest heaving with the effort to control the beast inside him. His jaw clenches, and for a moment, he almost looks like the man Elara fell in love with. But then the wolf roars inside him again, a terrible, guttural sound that tears through his throat. His hands shake as he reaches up to claw at his face, as though trying to tear the beast away, but it's too strong now. Too deep.

Kieran: (Voice low, full of anguish) I can't, Elara... I can't hold it back anymore. The wolf... it's too much. It's inside me, in my blood, in my soul. I've tried to run from it, but it's always been there. Always will be.

Elara's heart breaks at his words. She knows the pain he's in, the fear that has been eating away at him for years. She understands what he's saying—what he's feeling—but she refuses to accept it. Kieran isn't just the wolf. He's not defined by the curse that's trapped him for so long. She won't let him believe that. Not now, not when they're so close to breaking it.

Elara: (Shaking her head) No, Kieran. You're not just the wolf. You're more than that. You have a heart, you have a soul, and that's who I love. Don't let the darkness take that from you. Please, don't let it win.

Kieran's expression wavers as he looks at her, his eyes flickering with something close to despair. He wants to believe her. God, how he wants to believe her. But the wolf is powerful, and it's tearing him apart from the inside. He can feel it clawing at his chest, demanding freedom. The beast inside him is too strong to control now, too wild. He feels like he's slipping away, and all he can do is cling to the hope that Elara will still be there when it's all over.

Kieran: (Desperate) Elara… I don't know how much longer I can keep this up. The wolf is taking over. It's… it's too powerful.

The sound of his voice, strained and broken, cuts through Elara like a knife. She knows what he's asking—what he's really asking is for her to save him. But how can she save him when he's so far gone? The transformation is almost complete now, and she can see the wolf in him more clearly than ever. His body is twisting, his skin rippling with the fur that's spreading across his flesh. His teeth are lengthening, his nails turning into claws. And yet, in his eyes, there's still a flicker of the man he used to be.

The Breaking Point

Elara: (Firmly, stepping closer) I won't let go, Kieran. I won't. You're not alone. I'm right here with you.

Kieran's breath comes in sharp, erratic gasps as he stares at her, his eyes wild with fear. His body trembles violently as the change continues to overtake him, but he doesn't look away from Elara. There's something in his gaze, something vulnerable, something that makes her believe that the man he once was is still somewhere inside him, struggling to break free.

Kieran: (Whispering) I'm afraid, Elara. I'm afraid I'll lose myself. That the wolf will swallow me whole, and you'll never see me again. I won't be able to protect you. I won't be able to—

Before he can finish, the transformation surges through him, faster and more violently than before. His body buckles, and he screams—a terrifying, animalistic cry that echoes through the forest. His face distorts, his human features melting into the sharp, predatory angles of the wolf. Fur erupts from his skin, his hands turning into massive claws, and his eyes, once filled with uncertainty, are now fully consumed by the beast within him. But even in this state, there's a flicker of something in his eyes—something that still belongs to Kieran. Something that calls to her.

Elara steps forward without hesitation, her eyes locked on his. She doesn't flinch, doesn't pull away, even as the beast lunges toward her with a terrifying roar. She holds her ground, her heart pounding in her chest. This is it—the moment where everything changes. The moment where they either fall apart or find a way to save each other.

Elara: (Firmly) Kieran, listen to me! You're stronger than this! You can fight it! You've fought so much already—don't let the wolf win now!

Kieran's eyes flicker with recognition, but it's fleeting, almost as if the wolf is trying to push it down. The change is complete now—his body fully transformed into the beast that has haunted him for so long. But still, there's a part of him that hears her. A part of him that knows she's right. The wolf snarls, showing its teeth, but beneath it all, Kieran's voice can be heard, faint but clear.

Kieran: (Gravelly, struggling) I don't want to lose you, Elara. I don't want to hurt you.

The beast's growl rumbles in his chest, but Elara doesn't back down. She steps closer, her heart full of conviction.

Elara: (Softly) You won't hurt me, Kieran. I'm right here. I'll never leave you.

There's a long pause, the air thick with tension, as Kieran's claws hover inches from her skin. The transformation has made him a creature of nightmares, but in that moment, Elara can see the man he once was—the man who loved her, the man who fought so hard against the darkness that consumed him. And she knows that, if they can just hold on long enough, if they can just make it through this one final test, they can break the curse.

The Breaking Point

The wolf inside him snarls again, but this time it's not the same. This time, the anger and hunger are muted, as though something is holding it back. Kieran's body trembles, his massive form shaking as he fights for control. The air is thick with his struggle, the tension unbearable, and for a moment, Elara wonders if it's too late. But then, just as quickly, the tremor fades, and Kieran's eyes, still fierce and glowing with the wolf's power, soften.

Kieran: (Gravelly, barely a whisper) I can't... I can't do this alone, Elara.

Elara's heart skips a beat as she steps closer, her voice steady and full of love.

Elara: (Softly) You don't have to. I'm right here. We'll do this together.

For a moment, time seems to stand still, and the world holds its breath. The wolf inside Kieran growls once more, but the sound is weaker now, fading. The man inside is fighting back, pushing the darkness down, and Elara knows that they're on the verge of breaking the curse. But she also knows that the hardest part is still to come.

Kieran: (In a final, desperate whisper) I love you, Elara. I... I don't want to lose you.

Elara: (Tenderly) You won't lose me, Kieran. You never will.

And with those words, Kieran's body trembles one last time,

the last of the wolf's power fighting to break free. But Elara's touch is enough. The heart of the wolf is beginning to crack, and for the first time in his life, Kieran can see a way out. A way back to the man he was.

Seventeen

The Love That Binds

Scene 1: A Fragile Truce

The clearing is bathed in the cold, silver light of the moon, casting long shadows across the ground. The transformation is complete now, the wolf fully manifested in Kieran's form. His massive, fur-covered body is tense with the remnants of struggle, his claws digging into the earth, but the fire in his eyes is different now. There's a flicker of humanity within him, something Elara can see, even in the chaos of the beast that surrounds him. The air between them is thick with tension, and yet there's an undeniable bond that pulls them together—an invisible thread that neither the wolf nor the curse can sever.

Elara stands at the edge of the clearing, her breath shallow, her heart racing, but her resolve unshakable. She steps forward slowly, carefully, as though moving too quickly could shatter the fragile peace they've managed to form. Kieran's eyes track her every movement, his sharp, wolfish gaze following her with a mixture of caution and longing. The transformation hasn't just changed his body—it's changed him, broken him, twisted him in ways that make her wonder if the man she loves is still there at all.

Elara: (Softly, without hesitation) Kieran…

Kieran's ears twitch at the sound of her voice. His lips curl back slightly in a snarl, his body tensing as though ready to spring at her. But then, the snarl fades into a low growl, almost as if he's wrestling with himself. The wolf wants to attack, to dominate, but Kieran… Kieran doesn't want to hurt her.

Elara: (Stepping closer, her voice steady) Kieran, it's me. You don't have to fight anymore. We can stop this.

Kieran's eyes, dark and feral, flash with an emotion Elara can't quite place. It's a mix of confusion, anger, and something more vulnerable, something raw. The beast within him is still there, still raging, but beneath the surface, she sees Kieran—the man who has always been there for her, the man who has loved her through everything. She knows he's still in there, and she's not going to give up on him now.

Kieran: (Gravelly, his voice a mixture of human and beast) Elara… you don't understand. The wolf is part of me. It's always been. There's no escaping it. No… no controlling it.

The Love That Binds

Elara pauses, her heart aching with the weight of his words. She knows the truth in what he's saying—she knows the pain he's lived with, the fear of losing himself to the curse that binds him. But she also knows something else, something deeper. Love. And love, she believes, is the one thing powerful enough to break the chains that bind him.

Elara: (Gently, approaching him slowly) I understand more than you think. But love is stronger than any curse, Kieran. It always has been. You're not just the wolf. You are so much more. You are you. And that's what I love. The man who stood by my side, who fought for me, who gave everything to protect me.

Kieran's massive form trembles, his fur bristling with the raw energy of the transformation, but something in his eyes softens—just for a moment. He's fighting it. He's fighting himself, and Elara can see it. He doesn't want to lose her, but the fear of losing control is too great. The fear of hurting her is what keeps him from reaching out, from allowing himself to be vulnerable. He doesn't believe he deserves her love. He doesn't believe he's worth saving.

Kieran: (Barely a whisper) What if I hurt you, Elara? What if the wolf takes over completely? What if... what if I never come back to you?

Elara takes another step forward, her breath steady, her hands shaking slightly as she reaches out toward him. She can see the fear in his eyes—raw, unfiltered fear—and it breaks her heart. But she knows this is the only way. She has to reach him. She has to show him that she won't be scared away by the darkness, by the curse, or by the wolf inside him.

Elara: (Softly) You won't lose me. I won't let you. We've been through so much together, Kieran. This… this curse doesn't define you. Your heart does. And I know your heart. I know you.

For a moment, it seems as though Kieran might fall to his knees, the weight of his own emotions too much to bear. His large, wolfish frame quivers, as though the beast inside him is warring against the man. The air crackles with the intensity of the battle within him, but Elara doesn't flinch. She doesn't back down. She continues to move closer, her voice a steady beacon in the darkness.

Elara: (Whispering) You are stronger than this. You've always been strong. And you don't have to do this alone. You have me. We're in this together, Kieran. Always.

The wolf snarls, a primal sound that echoes through the forest, but there's something different about it now. It's not a roar of pure rage. It's a cry of frustration, of pain. Kieran's eyes flicker between the wolf's amber glow and the familiar, haunted green of the man she loves. She can see the battle in his eyes—he's so close to losing himself, to letting the wolf take over completely. But just as she's about to step forward again, something shifts within him. The transformation doesn't stop, but the snarl fades, replaced by a low, agonized whimper. The man inside him is still there. The wolf might be strong, but Kieran is stronger. And he's trying—he's trying so hard.

The Love That Binds

Elara: (Softly, her voice a gentle promise) I'm right here. I won't leave you, Kieran. No matter what happens, I'll be here. This isn't the end.

At her words, the transformation halts for a brief moment. Kieran's body stiffens, as though every muscle is locked in place, and then his eyes—the eyes that once belonged to the man she loved—meet hers. There's fear in them, yes, but there's also something else. Something tender. Something that's been buried for so long, hidden beneath the curse and the beast.

Kieran: (Hoarsely) Elara… I don't know if I can do this. I don't know if I can fight it any longer.

Elara's heart breaks at the vulnerability in his voice. She can see it now—see the weight of the burden he's carried all these years, the crushing fear that he might not make it. That the darkness inside him might win. But she won't let that happen. She won't let him fall into the abyss. Not now, not after everything they've been through.

Elara: (Reaching out to him, her hand trembling) You can. I believe in you. We've faced darkness together before, Kieran. This is no different. We can fight it. Together.

Kieran stares at her for a long moment, as if searching for the truth in her eyes. The wolf inside him still rages, still gnashes its teeth, but Elara's words cut through the chaos like a knife. She's right. He's not alone. He's never been alone. And he never will be, as long as she's by his side.

The Crying Wolf and the Darkest Night

Slowly, hesitantly, Kieran lowers his head, his massive form bending toward her, his hot breath ragged. His claws dig into the earth as he fights for control, his muscles trembling with the effort. The wolf inside him growls, protesting, but Kieran doesn't listen. Not anymore. He's not the wolf. He's not the curse. He's Kieran—the man who loves her.

Elara reaches out, her fingers brushing the side of his massive face. The touch is light, gentle, and for a moment, Kieran closes his eyes, surrendering to the warmth of her hand. The beast inside him still howls, but it's quieter now. The love between them is stronger than any curse. And in this moment, in the silence that follows, Kieran knows the truth.

He's not alone. He's never been alone.

Eighteen

The Ancient War

Scene 1: The Gathering Storm

The moon hangs high in the sky, casting its pale light over the crumbling ruins of an ancient temple, hidden deep in the heart of the forest. The wind howls through the trees, carrying with it a sense of impending doom. Elara stands before the entrance, her heart pounding in her chest. She feels the weight of the moment, the gravity of the choice that lies ahead. Kieran, still struggling with his curse, stands beside her, his posture rigid, the tension in his body palpable. The darkness around them seems to press in closer with each passing second, as though the very air is alive with an ancient malevolence.

Elara: (Softly, her voice trembling) This is where it all began, isn't it? The war. The curse. Everything.

The Crying Wolf and the Darkest Night

Kieran nods slowly, his eyes dark and distant. The memories are clear in his mind, haunting him, even now. The war that raged centuries ago—the battle between the werewolves and the creatures of the night, an eternal struggle that left nothing but ruin in its wake. It was in these very ruins that the curse was born, a twisted thing forged in blood and desperation. And now, after all this time, the war is about to reignite.

Kieran: (Grimly) Yes. This is where the pact was made. Where everything changed. The curse… it wasn't just about the transformation. It was about control. Power. And the price we had to pay to survive. I didn't know what I was getting into when I became part of this… this ancient war. But I should have. I should have known.

Elara turns to him, her eyes filled with understanding. She knows the burden he carries, the weight of history pressing down on him. But she also knows that he's stronger than he believes. She's seen him fight, seen him overcome impossible odds. And she refuses to let him carry this burden alone.

Elara: (Firmly) We can stop this, Kieran. We have the power to break the curse. Together.

Kieran looks at her, his eyes searching hers for a sign of certainty, for a sign that she truly believes they can succeed. The doubt is still there, lingering in the back of his mind, but the flicker of hope she ignites in him is undeniable.

Kieran: (Softly) I want to believe that, Elara. But this… this is bigger than us. This war, this curse—it's been going on for so

The Ancient War

long. There's so much at stake. And the enemy... they're not just creatures of the night. They're something else. Something ancient. Something that doesn't play by the rules.

Elara takes his hand, her grip firm and unyielding. She can feel the tremor in his touch, the uncertainty that still lingers in his heart. But she knows he's not a lost cause. She knows the strength he carries inside him, the strength of the man he used to be, the man she still believes in.

Elara: (Reassuringly) And we'll fight them. We'll fight whatever comes. Together. We're stronger than they realize. And you're stronger than you think.

Kieran looks at her, his eyes softening, the raw emotion that flickers behind them threatening to break through the walls he's built around himself. But before he can say anything, a low growl interrupts their moment of vulnerability. The air shifts, and the darkness around them deepens, as if the very forest itself is reacting to something ancient, something malevolent.

Kieran: (Low, tense) They're coming.

The ground trembles beneath their feet, and a faint whisper rides on the wind—a voice, barely audible, but filled with malice.

Voice: (Whispering, a hiss in the air) The bloodline is no longer pure. The curse will be your undoing.

Elara looks around, her eyes scanning the trees, her heart

pounding. She knows they're not alone. She can feel the presence of something dark, something watching them from the shadows. The air is thick with foreboding, as though the very forest is alive with ancient power. And then, from the depths of the temple, something stirs.

Kieran: (Grabbing her arm, pulling her back) Elara, get back! It's them!

Before Elara can react, a figure emerges from the darkness—tall, cloaked in shadows, its form barely visible. The figure moves with inhuman speed, its eyes glowing with a malevolent light. The air crackles with dark energy, and Elara feels the weight of the power it commands.

Elara: (Whispering) What… what are you?

The figure steps forward, its features still obscured by the cloak, but the voice that emanates from it is unmistakable—a voice that sends chills down her spine, a voice that feels ancient and filled with malice.

Figure: (Low, mocking) You dare challenge the ancient war? You are but children, playing in the shadows of things far beyond your understanding.

Kieran steps in front of Elara, his body tense, his eyes burning with the rage of the wolf that still resides within him.

Kieran: (Defiantly) I may be cursed, but I will fight. I will fight for the future. For Elara. And for everything we've lost.

The Ancient War

The figure tilts its head, a cruel smile playing at the corners of its lips.

Figure: (Amused) You think you can stop this, Kieran? The war has already begun. And it will end as it always does—with the blood of the unworthy. Your blood.

The figure raises its hand, and the air around them shifts. A powerful force crashes into Kieran, knocking him off his feet. He snarls, his claws extending, his body writhing as the wolf fights to take control. But Elara is quick to act. She reaches for him, pulling him back, her voice sharp and filled with command.

Elara: (Urgently) Kieran, don't! You have to control it. You're not alone in this!

Kieran's eyes meet hers, wild and filled with pain, but something in her gaze grounds him. He takes a deep breath, fighting against the surge of power that threatens to overtake him. The wolf within him howls in protest, but Kieran's resolve is stronger. He pushes the beast back, just enough to regain control.

Kieran: (Breathing heavily) I... I won't let it win. Not again.

The figure laughs, a deep, echoing sound that seems to reverberate through the temple. It steps forward, its eyes glowing with an unearthly light.

Figure: (Coldly) You cannot win, Kieran. The war has already been lost. And the curse you carry will be your undoing. You and your precious Elara… you will die here, in the ruins of the past.

Before Kieran can respond, a loud crash rings through the air, followed by the sound of rushing footsteps. More figures, cloaked in shadows, emerge from the forest, surrounding them. Elara's heart races as she looks around, but she doesn't falter. She won't let Kieran fight alone. She won't let him fall.

Elara: (Fiercely) We will not be your victims. We will fight. And we will win.

Kieran looks at her, the fire in his eyes burning brighter. For the first time in a long time, he feels the spark of hope. With Elara by his side, he can face anything. He can fight anything. Together, they are stronger than any curse, stronger than any war.

Kieran: (Gripping his claws, voice steady) Then let the war begin.

Nineteen

The Darkest Night

Scene 1: The Final Stand

The sky is a void, the blackness pressing in on every side as the storm clouds swirl overhead. The moon, once a silver beacon, is now obscured by the thick shroud of clouds, casting the world into an oppressive darkness. The wind howls like a beast, rattling the trees and bending the ancient ruins under the weight of an unseen force. Elara stands at the heart of the temple, her breath shallow, her hands trembling but steady. Beside her, Kieran is a shadow of the man he once was, the weight of the curse pressing down on him like a vice. His body trembles with the pull of the wolf, but his eyes—his eyes are filled with resolve.

Elara: (Quietly) Kieran, we can do this. You and me. Together. We've faced worse.

The Crying Wolf and the Darkest Night

Kieran's gaze flickers to her, the intensity of the battle raging behind his eyes. His fists clench, his body shifting between the form of a man and the animal he fears he's becoming. The wolf inside him howls, desperate for freedom, but Kieran keeps the beast at bay, only just. He's afraid. Afraid of losing control, of losing everything he's fought for.

Kieran: (Roughly) It's not the same. This... this war. It's not like before. This is darker, Elara. There's something else in the air tonight. Something older than the curse. Something that wants to end everything.

Elara steps forward, placing her hand gently on his arm. The contact is a lifeline—her warmth, her presence grounding him in the chaos that swirls around them. She knows what he's afraid of. She knows what's at stake. And she knows that this is the moment of truth. The moment when everything will either shatter or be made whole.

Elara: (Softly) We've always known what was at stake, Kieran. But we've never backed down. We won't back down now. I believe in you. I always have.

Kieran closes his eyes, the weight of her words washing over him. He draws in a shaky breath, trying to steady himself, but the pulse of the wolf calls to him, insistent, powerful. He feels it deep in his bones—the blood of his ancestors, the power of the curse, the pull of the ancient war. But he also feels her—Elara. She's the anchor that keeps him from being swallowed whole.

Kieran: (With difficulty) I don't know if I can do this. I don't

The Darkest Night

know if I can hold on much longer.

Elara: (Firmly) You're not alone. You never were.

Before Kieran can respond, the ground beneath them trembles, the air thick with malevolent energy. From the shadows of the temple, a figure emerges, cloaked in darkness. The creature's form is barely discernible, its presence overwhelming. A whisper of movement, the rustle of a cloak, and then its eyes—two orbs of red fire—lock onto them, filled with an ancient hatred. Elara steps back, instinctively pulling Kieran behind her, though she knows he's the one who will have to face this enemy.

Figure: (Coldly, with contempt) You think you can stop the darkness, child? You, who are bound by a curse you will never understand? You think your love will save you? Foolish. You are already dead.

The figure's voice echoes through the ruins, reverberating in Elara's chest like a cold wind. She shudders but refuses to let fear take hold. She looks at Kieran, her heart racing, but she doesn't flinch. They've come too far to turn back now. They've come too far to let the darkness win.

Elara: (Defiantly) We are not dead. We will not be your victims.

Kieran steps forward, his eyes blazing with the fire of his inner struggle. The wolf within him claws at the surface, snarling, but he holds it back, just barely. He's not sure how much longer he can control it, but one thing is clear—he will not let the ancient evil win. Not while he still has the strength to fight.

Kieran: (Low, growling) You can try to break us, but we won't be broken. We won't fall into the abyss you've created. This is where it ends.

The figure tilts its head, as if amused by their defiance. It steps forward, the cloak swirling around it like smoke, and its red eyes flash brighter. The very air seems to bend around it, twisting with dark power.

Figure: (Mocking) You speak of endings, but you do not know what you are up against. The war is ancient, Kieran. You were born into it, and you will die in it. It is the fate of all who carry the bloodline. The curse cannot be undone. The darkness cannot be stopped.

The ground shakes again, more violently this time, and the temple begins to crumble, the ancient stones cracking and shifting as if the very foundations are being torn apart. Elara stumbles, but Kieran catches her, his grip tight. He feels the pulse of the wolf within him, stronger now, demanding release. The darkness is closing in, the weight of the curse unbearable. But he can't let go. Not yet. Not while there's still a chance to fight.

Kieran: (Tense, struggling) I don't care how old this war is. I don't care how many curses have been cast. I'm not going to let it end like this. We will fight. We will win.

The figure's laughter rings out, high and hollow, filling the

The Darkest Night

night with an eerie resonance.

Figure: (Cynically) You are nothing. You are already lost. The blood of your ancestors is weak. The curse runs too deep. It cannot be undone, Kieran. The darkness will consume you. And your love? It will be the first to fall.

With a wave of its hand, the figure releases a surge of power so strong that it sends a shockwave through the temple. Elara is thrown to the ground, her vision spinning as she tries to regain her bearings. Kieran is knocked back, his body slamming into the stones with a sickening thud. The wolf inside him screams, clawing at his consciousness, but he forces it down, refusing to give in. Not now.

Elara: (Weakly, struggling to stand) Kieran!

Kieran's eyes snap open, his body trembling with the effort of keeping the wolf under control. He pushes himself to his feet, his muscles screaming in protest, but he doesn't stop. He can feel it—the darkness closing in, the curse tightening its grip. But there's something else, too. Something stronger. The love Elara has shown him, the faith she's placed in him, the strength they've shared. It gives him the will to fight, even when everything feels lost.

Kieran: (Shouting) Elara! Get up! We can't give up now!

Elara pushes herself to her knees, her breath ragged, but she doesn't hesitate. She rises to her feet, her resolve as fierce as ever. Together, they can face this. Together, they will defeat the darkness.

Elara: (Fiercely) We are not giving up. We are not lost. Not yet. Not while we still have a choice.

Kieran turns to face the figure once more, his body still trembling, but his resolve unwavering. The wolf howls inside him, but it's not a cry of desperation. It's a cry of defiance. Kieran knows that if he's going to win this battle, he can't do it alone. He needs Elara. He needs the love they share. He needs her belief in him.

Kieran: (With growing strength) You don't understand. You've underestimated us. You've underestimated me.

The figure's eyes narrow, its red glow intensifying.

Figure: (Snarling) Foolish. You still don't see. The war is already lost. You will die, just like the rest.

Kieran: (Shouting, with power) No. Not this time.

The air around them seems to crackle, the force of their words reverberating through the night. Elara stands by his side, her gaze unwavering, her heart steady. Together, they stand against the darkness. The war is not over yet.

The final battle begins.

Twenty

The Fall of the Beast

Scene 1: The Beast Revealed

The ground trembles beneath their feet, as if the earth itself is alive, rebelling against the chaos that has come to consume it. The air is thick with a heavy, foreboding presence, an ancient power that threatens to swallow everything in its path. The ruins of the temple loom around them, dark and twisted, their stones cracked and shattered as if they've borne witness to countless years of violence and bloodshed. In the distance, the sound of the wind howling through the trees is the only thing that breaks the oppressive silence.

Elara stands firm beside Kieran, her breath coming in sharp gasps. She can feel the tension building in the air, the imminent clash between life and death. Kieran's form is half-man, half-beast, his body trembling with the struggle for control. His eyes are wild, glowing with the ferocity of the wolf that is clawing its way to the surface. He's barely holding on, barely keeping the beast within him at bay. But as the dark figure approaches, Kieran knows that this will be the moment that defines them—whether they rise or fall.

Elara: (Quietly, with determination) Kieran, you have to hold on. Don't let it take you. We can do this. You can do this.

Kieran's gaze is distant, his focus lost somewhere between the man he used to be and the savage creature that threatens to consume him. He grits his teeth, a low growl escaping his throat as the wolf inside him fights for control. But Elara's voice—steady, full of conviction—reaches him like a lifeline, pulling him back from the brink. He takes a shaky breath, trying to steady his pulse, trying to quiet the monster within him.

Kieran: (With effort) I can't… I can't keep it in much longer, Elara. The wolf—it's too strong. The darkness—it's feeding on me.

Elara steps closer, her hand brushing against his. Her touch is a balm to his fractured spirit, reminding him of who he is, of the love that binds them together. She doesn't say anything at first, just holds his gaze, her eyes filled with an unwavering belief in him. The storm rages around them, but they are a singular force—united, unyielding.

Elara: (Softly) You are more than the curse, Kieran. You are more than the wolf. I believe in you. I always have.

The Fall of the Beast

Kieran's breath catches in his throat. Her words are like a beacon in the darkness, lighting a path he thought was lost forever. He feels the wolf inside him growl, its hunger, its rage threatening to tear him apart. But something stirs within him—something deep and ancient, a force that has been buried beneath the weight of the curse for far too long. It's the memory of who he was before all of this. It's the love they share.

Kieran: (Raggedly) I don't want to be this. I don't want to be a monster. I don't want to hurt you.

Elara's voice is unwavering as she steps even closer, her hand now resting gently on his chest, over his heart.

Elara: (Sincerely) You're not a monster, Kieran. You never were. You are a man who's been lost in the dark, but you don't have to stay there. You don't have to be alone.

Kieran's body shudders, the wolf inside him howling, clawing at the surface, but he holds it back with all his strength. The air around them seems to vibrate with the energy of their connection—the bond that's been forged through pain, through sacrifice, through love.

Kieran: (Barely a whisper) I don't know how much longer I can hold on.

But just as he says the words, the air shifts. The ground beneath them shakes, and the dark figure that has been watching them from the shadows steps forward, its presence more oppressive than ever. Its eyes gleam with malice, a cruel smile stretching across its face as it steps into the moonlight. Its form is no longer shrouded in mystery—it's a creature of pure darkness, its skin pale and slick, its eyes burning with a supernatural fire.

Figure: (Low and mocking) You still don't understand, do you, Kieran? The curse isn't just something you carry—it is you. The war is over. You are already defeated. There is no escape from this fate.

Kieran snarls, his hands shaking as he fights the beast within him. The curse, the war—it has all led to this moment. And though the odds are against them, though the darkness presses in from all sides, Kieran feels something stir in him—something greater than the curse. His will. His humanity.

Kieran: (Through gritted teeth) No. I'm not done yet.

The figure steps closer, its eyes never leaving Kieran. There is a hunger in those eyes, a dark hunger that promises nothing but destruction.

Figure: (Coldly) You can fight all you want. But the truth is, you are the beast. You always have been. The bloodline of your ancestors is nothing but a shadow. And in the end, the shadow will consume you. The darkness always wins.

With a swift motion, the figure raises its hand, and a wave of dark energy bursts forth, crashing toward Kieran and Elara. The force is overwhelming, the air thick with a malevolent power that threatens to tear them apart. Elara screams, but Kieran is already moving. The wolf surges within him, breaking free of the chains that held it in check. He growls, the sound primal and guttural, and with a roar, he charges toward the figure, his claws extended, his body shifting into the form of the beast.

Elara: (Desperate) Kieran! No!

But it's too late. Kieran is already caught in the thrall of the wolf, the creature fully awakened. His eyes glow with a feral light, and his body is no longer human. He is a beast, driven by hunger and rage. But even as the wolf takes over, a small part of him—the part that is still Kieran—remains, fighting to regain control.

Kieran: (Growling, his voice strained) I won't... let it... win!

The figure laughs, its voice a cruel, rasping sound that fills the night air with dread.

Figure: (Mocking) You think you can control it? You think you can choose between man and beast? There is no choice. You are the curse.

The figure reaches out, and the dark energy pulses, striking Kieran full force. He stumbles back, his body shaking, the pain of the attack nearly overwhelming him. The wolf inside him howls in agony, but Kieran holds on. He's not ready to fall. Not yet.

Kieran: (Roaring) I am more than the curse! I am Kieran! I am not just the wolf!

The Crying Wolf and the Darkest Night

With a final, desperate push, Kieran throws himself forward, his claws slashing through the air, connecting with the figure's chest. The creature staggers back, a hiss of pain escaping its lips as it tries to regain its balance. But Kieran doesn't stop. He presses forward, the wolf's power coursing through him, the sheer force of his will driving him onward.

Elara watches in awe and fear, her heart racing as she sees the struggle unfold before her. Kieran is battling not just the figure, but the darkness within himself. She knows that this is the moment—either he succumbs to the beast, or he overcomes it once and for all.

Elara: (Shouting) Kieran! You can do it! You're stronger than this!

Kieran's body trembles, his claws sinking deeper into the figure's chest. The creature snarls, but it's weakening. Kieran's eyes flash with a fierce determination. The darkness is strong, but he is stronger.

Kieran: (Fiercely) You're right about one thing… the darkness is strong. But it can't win. Not when I have something worth fighting for.

With one final, earth-shattering roar, Kieran pulls the figure into the light, his claws tearing through its heart. The creature shrieks in agony, its body writhing and convulsing as the dark energy that sustains it begins to unravel. The figure's form flickers, its power dissipating, until, with a final scream, it crumbles to dust.

The Fall of the Beast

Kieran stands over the ashes of the beast, panting, his body shaking with the exertion of the battle. His eyes are still glowing with the remnants of the wolf's power, but they slowly fade back to their normal hue as the beast inside him recedes. The curse is not gone, but for the first time in his life, Kieran feels something different—something powerful. A freedom that's been denied to him for so long.

Elara steps forward, her hand reaching for him. He takes it, his grip strong, his heart still pounding in his chest.

Elara: (Softly) You did it. You beat it. You beat the beast.

Kieran looks at her, the weight of everything they've been through settling in. He's tired. He's broken. But he's also whole, in a way he never thought possible. The wolf's howl has fallen silent, and in its place, there's a new kind of peace.

Kieran: (Quietly) We did it. Together.

They stand in the ruins of the temple, the darkness that has plagued them finally lifted. But as the wind dies down, as the last echoes of the battle fade away, a new day begins to rise on the horizon—a day of hope, of redemption, of a future they will build together.

Twenty-One

A Heart's Sacrifice

Scene 1: The Aftermath of Victory

The dawn breaks over the shattered landscape, a pale light filtering through the ruins of the ancient temple. The air is still thick with the remnants of battle—the burnt scent of the beast's ashes, the faint smell of blood, the echoes of the struggle that has just passed. Kieran and Elara stand together, side by side, but there's a distance between them, a quiet tension in the air. The world seems to hold its breath, as if waiting for something more.

Kieran's eyes, though still sharp and alert, are weary. The wolf inside him is quiet for now, but the battle has taken its toll. His body aches, and the scars of the curse are still fresh. He feels the weight of his past pressing on him, the echoes of the man he used to be blending with the creature he's fought so hard

A Heart's Sacrifice

to suppress. He turns to Elara, his gaze soft, yet filled with something that is far more complex than gratitude.

Kieran: (Hoarsely) Elara... I don't know how to thank you. I don't know how to say what you've done for me.

Elara stands beside him, her expression unreadable, though her eyes shine with an emotion that mirrors his. Her hands are still trembling, but not from fear—no, it's from the intensity of what they've just been through, the bond that has grown between them. Her voice is steady, though the weight of her words lingers in the air.

Elara: (Gently) You don't have to thank me, Kieran. We did this together. We're still here, aren't we?

She looks at him, her eyes searching his face as if trying to read something that's hidden deep within. Kieran's heart races, though it's not from the threat of the beast anymore. There's something more—a tension that isn't physical, but emotional. A truth that has been left unsaid for far too long. Elara takes a step closer, her voice low, almost a whisper.

Elara: (Softly) But I need to know something, Kieran. After all of this, after everything we've been through—what happens now?

Kieran's heart skips a beat. He knows what she's asking, but the question feels heavier than anything he's ever faced before. The world has shifted around them, and now, in the calm after the storm, the future is uncertain. He wants to tell her that everything will be fine, that they've won, and they can move on. But deep down, he knows the truth is far more complicated than that.

Kieran: (Struggling for words) I don't know. I don't know what comes next. All I've ever known is the curse... the wolf... the fight. I don't even know who I am without it anymore.

Elara's gaze softens, her hand reaching out to touch his arm, grounding him. She can see the internal battle raging within him—the man he once was, the beast he's tried to suppress, and the love they share. It's all tangled together, inseparable, and she knows that the journey isn't over, not yet.

Elara: (Gently) Then let me help you find out. We'll figure it out together. But I need to know that you're ready to face what's ahead.

Kieran's eyes meet hers, and for a moment, it's as if time stands still. The world around them seems to fade, and all that exists is the bond between them. He reaches for her hand, his grip firm and steady, but there's an undercurrent of fear in his chest, something he can't quite shake off.

Kieran: (Quietly) I don't deserve you, Elara. After everything I've done, after everything I've become... I don't deserve to be happy. Not after all the pain I've caused.

Elara shakes her head, her eyes never leaving his. Her voice is filled with quiet strength, a tenderness that cuts through the confusion and doubt in his heart.

A Heart's Sacrifice

Elara: (Solemnly) You've suffered enough, Kieran. We've both suffered enough. It's time to choose something else. It's time to choose each other. To choose life, together.

Kieran looks at her, his heart heavy with the weight of her words. He feels the wolf within him stir once more, but this time, it's not out of rage. It's the same primal hunger—the hunger for something more than survival, for something he thought he'd lost forever.

Kieran: (Softly) What if it's too late? What if the wolf never truly leaves?

Elara looks up at him, her eyes full of conviction. She steps closer to him, her heart racing in her chest. She knows what it costs to face this truth, to face the possibility that the wolf will always be a part of him. But she also knows that the love they share is worth the risk. It's worth everything.

Elara: (Quietly) I'm not asking you to be perfect, Kieran. I'm asking you to be real. To be with me, as you are. And I will be here, no matter what.

For a moment, there's nothing but silence. The words hang in the air, heavy with promise. Kieran stands still, trying to find a way to put his tumultuous feelings into words, but the more he thinks about it, the more he realizes that there's nothing more to say. Elara has already given him the answer. She's chosen him. And in this moment, he chooses her, too.

Kieran: (Whispering) I don't know how to love you the way

you deserve, Elara. But I'll try. I'll try with everything I have.

Elara smiles softly, her heart swelling with emotion. She leans forward, her lips brushing against his in a tender kiss. It's a kiss filled with years of pain, of sacrifice, but also with hope. Hope for a future they will build together, a future that's no longer defined by the curse, the darkness, or the wolf.

Scene 2: The Sacrifice

But as they pull away from the kiss, there's a shadow in the distance. A presence that's unfamiliar, but unmistakable. It's a figure, moving toward them through the mist. And though Elara doesn't sense it at first, Kieran's instincts flare. His hand tightens on her wrist as he looks toward the approaching figure, his heart beginning to race once more.

Kieran: (Hissing) Stay back, Elara.

The figure steps forward, its silhouette emerging from the fog. The face is obscured, but there's something about the way it moves—something predatory, something dark.

Figure: (Coldly) You think you're free, Kieran? You think you've won? The curse does not die so easily.

Elara looks up at Kieran, her face filled with confusion and concern.

Elara: (Urgently) Who are you? What do you want?

A Heart's Sacrifice

The figure steps closer, its eyes gleaming with malice. It doesn't answer her, but its presence is enough to send a chill down their spines.

Figure: (Malevolently) You think the darkness is gone? You think it's over? The price of the curse is more than you realize, Kieran. And I've come to collect.

Kieran's blood runs cold. He can feel the truth, the weight of it pressing down on him. The curse, the wolf, the battle—they've all been leading to this moment. The end isn't here yet. And neither is the beginning of their peace.

Kieran: (With quiet dread) What price? What do you want from us?

The figure doesn't speak for a long moment. But when it does, its voice is filled with the weight of inevitability.

Figure: (Darkly) A heart. A sacrifice. You knew this day would come, Kieran. And it will be your heart—your humanity—that pays the cost.

Elara gasps as the realization hits her like a wave. She looks up at Kieran, her eyes wide with fear.

Elara: (Pleading) No… please. Don't say that. Kieran, don't do this. There's always another way.

Kieran looks at her, his heart breaking, but the truth is already clear in his mind. His hand tightens on hers, the weight of the decision pressing down on him like a thousand stones.

Kieran: (Softly) Elara... I love you. But this is my burden to bear. I always knew it would come to this.

The figure steps forward, a wicked smile curling on its lips as it reaches for Kieran's heart.

Elara: (Desperate) Kieran! No!

Kieran's eyes lock with hers for one final, heartbreaking moment. He knows the sacrifice he's about to make, but it's the only way to end the curse. To save her. To save them all.

Kieran: (Whispering) I love you, Elara. Always.

With that, he steps into the figure's grasp, knowing that this will be the last choice he ever makes.

Twenty-Two

The Moon's Last Gaze

Scene 1: The Final Decision

The moon hangs high in the sky, casting an eerie glow over the ruins where the battle had once raged. The air is still now, pregnant with the heavy silence of what's to come. Kieran stands before the looming figure, his heart pounding in his chest, each beat a reminder of the choice he is about to make. Elara stands just behind him, her breath shallow, eyes wide with fear. She doesn't understand yet, doesn't know what Kieran has already realized—the sacrifice that must be made to truly break the curse.

Kieran's hands tremble, but it's not out of fear. It's the weight of his love for her, for everything they've fought for, pressing down on him. The figure before him, cloaked in shadows, is an embodiment of everything Kieran has fought against. But it's also something he can't escape. Not now.

Elara's voice cuts through the tense silence, filled with desperation.

Elara: (Pleading) Kieran, no. Please, you can't do this. There's always another way. We can figure it out together. There has to be another way!

Kieran's eyes meet hers, but the depth of his gaze is unreadable, filled with sorrow, yet something else—something resolute. His heart aches as he watches her face contort with worry and confusion, the love they share written clearly in every line of her expression.

Kieran: (Voice cracking) Elara, I've tried to escape this for so long. I've run from the wolf inside me, from the darkness that's followed me for years. But now... now it's time to end it. To make sure it never rises again.

The figure's laugh is soft, sinister—a whisper that curls around Kieran's mind, seeping into the depths of his soul.

Figure: (Mockingly) You think you can stop it, Kieran? You think this sacrifice will rid you of your curse? You are a fool. The wolf will never leave you. Not entirely.

Elara steps forward, her voice shaking but determined.

Elara: (Fiercely) No. You're wrong. He's stronger than that. We're stronger than that. We've already fought through so much, and we will find another way. We won't let you take him.

The figure's eyes gleam with malice, and for a moment, it feels like the world is holding its breath. The winds shift, stirring the dust of the battle, as if the earth itself is waiting for Kieran's decision.

Kieran turns slowly, his eyes searching Elara's face. Her words sting, a reminder of what they've lost already—the battles fought, the lives torn apart. But her strength, her unwavering belief in him, shakes something deep inside him. He doesn't want to leave her. Not like this. But the weight of the curse is too much to bear.

Kieran: (Softly, with finality) I don't want to hurt you, Elara. I don't want to be this creature anymore. But to end the curse, I must make the ultimate sacrifice. And if it means saving you—saving us all—then it is a price I must pay.

Elara steps forward, her hand reaching out to touch his arm, her voice trembling but fierce.

Elara: (Desperate) No, Kieran. I won't let you. You're not alone in this anymore. You never were. If you sacrifice yourself, then what's left for me? What's left for us? We promised we'd be together, through everything. You don't have to do this.

For a brief moment, Kieran closes his eyes, the weight of her words crashing over him. Her love, her faith in him—it cuts deeper than any wound he's ever suffered. But there's something darker, something that can't be ignored, clawing at his heart. The figure before him, the embodiment of his curse, is right in one thing—he cannot outrun what he is. And perhaps, in this moment, the only way to truly escape the darkness is to embrace the ultimate truth.

Kieran: (Whispering) I wish I could say I could run away with you, Elara. But I've spent so long hiding from this, from myself. I need to face it. This is the only way.

As the figure approaches, its eyes narrowing in satisfaction, Elara grabs Kieran's hand, pulling him back toward her. She doesn't understand. Not fully. But she won't let him go without a fight.

Elara: (Tearfully) You're not alone, Kieran. Don't let this thing win. Don't let it take you from me. I love you. We will find another way.

Kieran's heart pounds, the wolf inside him stirring, tugging at his every fiber. The beast is restless, but he's determined to keep it at bay, for her. But the pull of the moon, of the curse, is strong. He knows it's a battle he may not win.

Figure: (Sneering) You think love can save you? You think this weakness will set you free? The curse does not care for love, for promises. It cares only for what it demands.

The figure steps closer, its form flickering in and out of shadow. The air grows thick with its presence, the darkness curling around them like a serpent. But in the stillness of that moment, Kieran hears something—a whisper. It's faint, almost imperceptible, but it's there.

A voice. His voice. From the past.

Voice: (Whispering) You can be free, Kieran. You can be free of the beast. But it will cost you everything.

Kieran's chest tightens as the words cut through him like a blade. He knows this voice—it is the voice of his past, of the man he once was before the curse took hold of him. And now, it seems that voice has returned to haunt him one last time.

Kieran: (Muttering, to himself) Everything... it always comes back to this. The cost.

The figure watches him, its smile twisted with malice. Elara looks between them, sensing the shift in the air, sensing that something is changing within Kieran.

Elara: (Urgently) Kieran, please! This is not you. You don't have to listen to it. We can fight this together. Don't give in to the darkness.

But Kieran's eyes are locked on the figure, his body tense, the transformation beginning to take root again. The pull of the moon, of the curse, is undeniable. His body aches, his muscles shift and tense, but his mind is still with her, still with the love that binds them. He can feel the wolf inside him stirring—no longer a separate entity, but a part of him, something he can't escape.

Kieran: (Barely audible) I'm sorry, Elara. I don't know if I can stop it. I don't know if I can win this fight.

Elara's hand reaches out again, her fingers brushing against his, and in that moment, their eyes meet. A silent understanding passes between them. There's no more time. She can feel the weight of the decision, too—the sacrifice that's hanging over them both.

Elara: (Softly) Whatever happens, Kieran… I will always love you.

Kieran's heart shatters at her words. He wants to fight, to refuse what the curse demands, but deep down, he knows it's the only way. The only way to ensure that they both survive this night. The only way to free them from the shadows.

Kieran: (Voice breaking) I don't want to leave you. I don't want to say goodbye.

The figure steps forward, its hands reaching for Kieran's chest. It's time.

Elara: (Whispering) You don't have to say goodbye. You never will.

Kieran's heart races, and with one final, desperate breath, he steps into the figure's grasp. His chest aches, his breath shallow as the figure's hands wrap around him, pulling him into the darkness. But just before the world collapses into oblivion, he feels it—a warmth, a connection, stronger than anything he's ever known.

The moon above seems to pulse with an ethereal light, bathing them in its silver glow. The curse is ending. The darkness is receding. But at what cost?

Kieran's eyes close, and the world goes black.

Twenty-Three

The Return of the Shadows

Scene 1: The Quiet Before the Storm

The air feels different now, as if the world has held its breath for too long. Elara stands alone on the battlefield, the ruins of the fight still scattered across the desolate ground. The moon, full and glowing, watches from above. Its light is both comforting and haunting, casting long, creeping shadows across the land. Everything is eerily silent. Kieran is gone, his sacrifice weighing heavily on her heart.

Elara's hand trembles as she reaches down to touch the ground where Kieran had fallen. The earth is cold, and yet, she feels a heat emanating from the depths of it. Something is stirring—something old and powerful. A faint whisper echoes in the wind, too soft to understand, but loud enough to send chills crawling up her spine.

The Return of the Shadows

Elara: (Whispering) Kieran… where are you? Please, tell me you didn't leave me alone.

Her voice cracks as tears begin to blur her vision, but she wipes them away angrily. She cannot afford weakness—not now. The shadows, the curse, they are still out there, still waiting for their chance to rise again. And as much as she wants to grieve, she knows the battle is far from over.

Suddenly, the wind shifts. The ground rumbles beneath her feet, and a shadow breaks through the moonlight. It's dark, deeper than the night itself. A silhouette emerges from it—tall, cloaked in a shroud of darkness, its form barely visible but undeniably menacing. Elara's breath catches in her throat as she instinctively steps back, her hand reaching for the dagger at her waist.

Elara: (Hissing) Who are you?

The figure doesn't speak, but its presence is enough to answer the question. It is the same darkness that had plagued Kieran's soul, the same malevolent force that had sought to destroy everything they held dear. The curse is not gone—not completely. Elara knows it now. The shadows are back, and they've come to reclaim what was taken from them.

The figure steps closer, the air growing colder with every movement. Elara's heart races, her mind spinning. She is alone, unprepared for what is coming. But she cannot retreat—not when she knows what's at stake.

The Crying Wolf and the Darkest Night

Elara: (Gripping her dagger tightly) Get away from me. I won't let you take him. Not again.

The figure's form shudders, shifting in a way that makes Elara's skin crawl. Then, it speaks—its voice like a thousand whispers, distorted and full of menace.

Figure: (Softly) You think you can stop what's coming? You think you can defy the shadows? Kieran may have fallen, but the beast has not been vanquished. It is only waiting... for its return.

Elara takes a step back, eyes wide, her breath shallow. The words hit her like a physical blow. The beast is still here. The curse is not over. The shadowed figure steps closer still, its presence suffocating, and a sense of dread rises in her chest.

Elara: (Stammering) No. I—I won't let you—Kieran can't be... I won't lose him!

The figure laughs, its voice hollow and echoing in the cold air. There is no humor in it, only darkness and the promise of destruction.

Figure: (Chuckling darkly) You misunderstand, girl. Kieran's fate was sealed the moment he embraced the beast. The curse does not end with a death. It lives on, waiting to reclaim what is rightfully its own.

Elara's heart races, panic beginning to claw at her chest. She can feel the weight of the figure's words, and a cold knot forms in her stomach. Kieran's sacrifice had been a desperate plea to end it all—but had it truly worked? Was there really no hope left?

The figure steps forward, its movements fluid, impossibly fast. Elara raises her dagger, but it's too slow. The shadow's hand grips her wrist with inhuman strength, and she gasps in pain as the dagger falls to the ground.

Figure: (Hissing) You cannot stop this. You are merely a pawn in a game far older than you can understand. You think you know loss, but you have no idea what true darkness is.

Elara struggles, trying to break free from the figure's hold, but it only tightens its grip. The air grows colder still, and her breath comes in sharp, ragged gasps. A sharp pain shoots through her arm as the figure squeezes harder, its fingers like ice.

Elara: (Grimacing) Let go of me... let go of him...

The figure's face remains hidden beneath the cloak, but its voice deepens, growing even more ominous as it speaks again.

Figure: (Low, menacing) You cannot fight what is destined. The curse was never meant to be broken by love, by sacrifices. It was meant to consume, to devour everything. And soon... it will consume you as well.

The grip loosens just slightly as the figure tilts its head, studying Elara with an unsettling calm. Then, its voice grows softer, almost coaxing.

Figure: (Softly) You are so strong, Elara. But you cannot stop it. You cannot stop what is coming. The shadows will rise. The moon will wax once more, and Kieran… Kieran will return, but not as the man you knew. No. He will return as the beast, and this time, he will belong to the darkness forever.

Elara's heart skips a beat. The figure's words resonate deep within her, stirring something primal in her. She refuses to believe it, refuses to accept the idea that everything they fought for—the love they shared, the battles they won—was for nothing. She will not allow the darkness to claim him again.

Elara: (Defiantly) No. You're lying. I won't let you twist the truth. Kieran… Kieran is not lost. He is not a monster. You will not have him.

The figure steps back, almost amused by her defiance. Its eyes gleam with a predatory satisfaction as it watches her.

Figure: (Coldly) You still do not understand. The shadows do not lie. They simply exist. And soon, you will understand their truth.

The wind picks up, the shadows growing thicker as the figure fades into the night, its form dissipating like smoke. Elara stands frozen in the center of the battlefield, her breath quick and shallow. The world feels like it's slipping away from her, the sense of dread overwhelming her. But there is one thing she knows for certain—Kieran is not lost. Not yet.

She drops to her knees, her heart aching as she whispers his name, her voice barely audible over the wind.

Elara: (Whispering) Kieran… I will find you. I will bring you back. No matter the cost.

Scene 2: The Unseen War

The moon hangs high, casting a long shadow over the ruins, and in the distance, Elara can hear the faint sound of howls rising in the night. A distant, mournful cry that cuts through her like a knife. It is Kieran, or at least the remnants of him—calling out from the depths of the curse.

Elara stands, wiping her tears away, her resolve hardening. She cannot waste time in despair. The shadows are returning, and she must act quickly. The hunt for Kieran, for his humanity, is not over. It's only just begun.

She turns toward the horizon, determination burning in her eyes. No matter what the shadows promise, no matter the cost, Elara will face the darkness. She will find the light in the deepest night.

And she will fight until the very last breath to bring Kieran back from the edge of the abyss.

Twenty-Four

The Reckoning

~~~

Scene 1: The Echoes of Despair

The night is heavy with a tangible silence, an eerie calm that seems to have settled over the world like a suffocating blanket. Elara walks alone through the darkened woods, her footsteps muffled by the thick carpet of fallen leaves. Her heart beats in time with the rising tension in the air, a feeling that something vast and terrible is approaching. Her breath comes in shallow gasps, the cold seeping into her skin, but it is the gnawing sense of dread that truly chills her to the bone.

She clenches her fists, the memory of the shadowed figure's words still echoing in her mind—words that gnaw at her resolve, words that twist the knife of doubt deeper into her chest.

The Reckoning

Figure: (Echoing) You cannot stop what is coming. The shadows will rise... and Kieran will return. But not as the man you knew. He will return as the beast, and he will belong to the darkness forever.

Elara halts, the weight of the figure's words pressing down on her like a physical force. She closes her eyes, her hand resting on the hilt of the dagger at her side, a reminder of the promises she's made and the love that drives her. She will not believe it. She refuses to.

Elara: (Softly to herself) No... Kieran isn't lost. I know him... I know his heart. And I will find him. I will bring him back.

She opens her eyes, determination flickering in their depths. But deep inside, a seed of fear has been planted, and it begins to sprout, feeding on her uncertainty. How could she be so sure? The beast, the darkness—it was real. And if what the figure said was true, how much longer would Kieran remain the man she loved?

The wind picks up again, rustling the trees around her, but it doesn't soothe her. If anything, it feels like a warning. The hairs on the back of her neck stand on end as the distant howl rises again, louder this time, full of pain and primal fury. It is unmistakable. It is Kieran.

Elara's heart leaps in her chest, but the sound is not one of hope. It is a cry of torment, a cry that tears at her very soul. The howl is filled with rage, despair, and something darker—something that chills her to the core.

Elara: (Whispering) Kieran…

She doesn't waste another second. She begins to run, her legs pumping furiously beneath her as she pushes through the dense trees, heedless of the branches that snap against her skin. The howl echoes in her ears, guiding her, but also torturing her, a reminder of the beast he could become. She will reach him. She has to.

Scene 2: The Wolf's Lair

The forest seems to stretch on forever, the path growing narrower, more twisted as Elara pushes deeper into its heart. The air grows colder with every step, and she can feel the presence of something ancient lurking in the shadows. The howl is louder now, closer—her pulse races as she bursts through a thicket of trees and stumbles into a clearing.

There, in the center of the clearing, is the last place she would ever have expected to find herself—the heart of the cursed woods. The place where it all began. The place where Kieran's fate had been sealed. The moon hangs low and full in the sky, its light casting long, sharp shadows that seem to move and writhe on their own. The earth is cracked, the ground scarred by some ancient, unseen force.

And there, standing in the middle of it all, is Kieran.

Elara's breath catches in her throat as she freezes, taking in the sight before her. Kieran is on his knees, his head bowed, his back hunched as if he's carrying an invisible weight. His

The Reckoning

clothes are torn, his hair wild, but it's the look in his eyes—the emptiness, the pain—that sends a spike of terror through her heart.

Elara: (Shouting) Kieran!

At the sound of her voice, Kieran lifts his head. His eyes—his once warm, loving eyes—are now nothing more than pools of blackness, void of humanity. He snarls, his lips curling back to reveal sharp, gleaming fangs. A low growl rumbles from deep within his chest, and for a moment, Elara fears she's lost him. He's become the monster she feared. The beast he had fought so hard to control is finally free.

But then, he speaks. His voice is a broken whisper, barely audible over the howling wind.

Kieran: (Hoarsely) Elara... you shouldn't have come.

Elara steps forward, her eyes never leaving his. Her heart aches at the sight of him—at the darkness that has consumed him, and yet, she can still see the remnants of the man she loves in his tortured expression.

Elara: (Softly) I couldn't stay away. I couldn't leave you. Kieran, you're still in there. I know you are. Please, fight it. Fight the curse. You can't give up now. Not after everything.

Kieran's body trembles, his hands gripping the earth as if he's trying to hold on to some semblance of control. His breath comes in ragged gasps, and his eyes flicker with a mixture of pain and longing as he looks at her.

Kieran: (Desperate) I can't... it's too strong. Elara, I— (Pauses, his voice trembling) I've lost control. The beast inside of me, it... it's too much. I can't hold it back. I—I don't want to hurt you.

Elara's chest tightens as she takes another step closer, reaching her hand out toward him. Her fingers tremble as they hover just inches from his skin.

Elara: (Pleading) You won't hurt me. I know you, Kieran. I know the man you are. You're not the beast. You're not this... thing. Please. Please, come back to me. Let me help you.

Kieran's eyes close tightly, as though the very thought of giving in to her words causes him physical pain. He gasps, his body shaking violently as if he's struggling to suppress the animal inside of him. He tries to speak again, but the words are choked, forced through clenched teeth.

Kieran: (Growling) I can't! Elara... you don't understand! The curse... it's too powerful! It's breaking me!

Elara takes one more step forward, her heart in her throat, her hand now trembling just inches from his face. She can feel the heat of him, the frantic energy radiating from his body, and it terrifies her—but she cannot stop herself. Not now. She cannot lose him.

Elara: (Tearfully) I understand more than you know. I won't

The Reckoning

let you do this alone. I won't let you become the thing you fear. You're not alone, Kieran. You never have been. I'm right here. Fight for us. Fight for the love we have. Please.

Kieran's eyes flicker with something—something deeper than the madness that churns within him. A spark of recognition. A spark of hope. But just as quickly, it's gone. His body shifts, his spine arching as the transformation begins, his fingers lengthening into claws. His face contorts, the beast within him fighting to break free.

Kieran: (Snarling) I don't want this… I don't want to hurt you!

Elara lunges forward, her hand finally reaching his face, her fingers brushing his skin. It's like touching fire—his body is burning, and yet she doesn't pull away. She holds on, holding onto him with everything she has left.

Elara: (Whispering) I'm not afraid of you, Kieran. I'm not afraid. I love you.

For a moment, there's a pause—a breath, a beat of silence. And then, something shifts within Kieran. His body shudders, and his eyes flicker back to the man she knows, the man she loves. The beast roars in protest, but it's quieter now, more distant. Kieran is fighting back.

Kieran: (Hoarsely) Elara… I… I don't know how much longer I can hold it back.

Elara: (Determined) You can. You will. I'm with you, Kieran.

The Crying Wolf and the Darkest Night

Always.

And for the first time in what feels like an eternity, Elara sees the man she loves—fragile, broken, but still fighting—staring back at her, his humanity not yet lost to the darkness.

Twenty-Five

The Dawn of a New Moon

Scene 1: The Calm Before the Storm

The moon hangs low in the sky, casting its pale light across the still forest. The wind stirs the trees in an eerie whisper, but the air itself is heavy, as though holding its breath. Elara stands with Kieran, their hands locked together in a fragile truce. The clearing around them is quiet now, save for the distant rustling of leaves and the faintest rustle of the earth beneath their feet. The tension, thick with unspoken fear, lingers between them like a dark cloud.

Kieran's transformation has halted, his claws retracting into human fingers, but his body still trembles with the remnants of the beast's fury. His eyes, though no longer completely black, still flicker with an unsettling darkness, a reflection of the battle within him. Elara can feel it—the weight of the curse that he

The Crying Wolf and the Darkest Night

fights against, a force so powerful it has nearly torn them apart.

Elara: (Softly) We need to move. The danger isn't over. Whatever happens… we can't stay here. Not now.

Kieran's gaze flickers to the sky, where the last sliver of the full moon hangs precariously, moments away from descending behind the horizon. He nods, but his face is pale, drained from the struggle, and the fear of what is to come still holds him captive.

Kieran: (Voice tight) I can feel it… the curse. It's not gone. The moon isn't done with me yet.

Elara steps closer, her hand resting gently on his arm. She doesn't say anything at first. She simply watches him, her heart aching with a love so fierce, so unyielding, it feels as though it could shatter under the weight of the world. He's not just a man to her—he's a part of her, and she knows, deep in her bones, that she cannot—and will not—let him succumb to this fate.

Elara: (Firmly) We will face it together, Kieran. You don't have to fight this alone. I'm here. Always. You said it yourself—love is our strength. We've come this far. We can do this.

Kieran looks down at her, his eyes softening for a moment, the light of hope flickering faintly behind the storm of fear. But then, the howl rises again—louder now, a tortured cry that echoes through the trees, sending a ripple of terror through Elara's chest.

The Dawn of a New Moon

Elara: (Tensely) What is that? That sound...

Kieran's face hardens again, his features drawn tight with pain and dread.

Kieran: (Whispering) The beast. The darkness. It's not just the curse, Elara. There's something else out there. Something that is using the curse, manipulating it. Something ancient... and cruel.

As if to prove his words, the wind picks up again, howling with a sudden fury. The trees bend beneath the force, their branches reaching toward the ground like desperate hands. The sound of snapping twigs and the rustle of something large moving through the underbrush fills the air. Elara's heart pounds in her chest, but she does not flinch. She stands tall, unwavering.

Elara: (Resolute) What do we do now?

Kieran turns, his gaze scanning the shadows of the forest. The last remnants of the moon are slipping away, vanishing behind the darkening sky. He feels the pull of the curse, the hunger of the beast inside him, and the looming presence of something far worse than he has ever faced.

Kieran: (With finality) We face it head-on. Whatever this is, whatever it's doing to me, we end it tonight. We have to stop it—before it destroys us both.

Scene 2: The Beast Within

Elara moves to stand beside him, her gaze fixed on the shifting shadows ahead, her senses heightened as though the very forest is holding its breath. The air is thick, heavy with the scent of earth and decay, and yet there is something else in the air, something old and ancient, like the very bones of the earth have stirred beneath their feet.

Kieran's hands clench into fists, his nails digging into his palms as the pull of the transformation grows stronger with every passing second. His body shifts slightly, muscles bulging as the bones beneath his skin protest, the curse fighting against his control. He feels the beast, deep within his chest, clawing to be released. He can't keep it at bay much longer.

Kieran: (Hissing through clenched teeth) Elara… you need to go. Get out of here. I can't hold it back for much longer. This isn't a fight you can win.

Elara shakes her head, her eyes unwavering as she steps closer, her hand brushing against his arm, grounding him, tethering him to the world that still has a place for him. He is not lost yet. He will not be lost.

Elara: (Determined) I'm not leaving you. Not this time.

Kieran's breath is ragged now, and his muscles twitch with the urge to transform. His mind is a battlefield, a constant war between the man he is and the beast threatening to consume him. He looks at Elara, her presence a fragile anchor in the storm of his torment.

The Dawn of a New Moon

Kieran: (Desperate) Elara, you don't understand! If I lose control—if the beast fully awakens—it won't be me you're fighting. It will be something far worse. Something you can't defeat.

The howl comes again, louder this time, closer, almost deafening. And then, from the darkness of the woods, a figure emerges—a tall, imposing silhouette with eyes glowing an eerie amber, the scent of death and decay emanating from it like a cloud of poison. The figure steps into the clearing, its features hidden in shadow, but its presence unmistakable. It is not human. It is the true source of the curse, the thing that has been manipulating Kieran's fate all along.

Elara: (Staring at the figure) Who… who are you?

The figure steps forward, its voice a low, rasping growl that seems to reverberate through the ground beneath them.

Figure: (Darkly) I am the one who has been waiting for this moment. The one who has shaped your fate, Kieran. And yours, Elara.

Kieran's eyes widen as he steps protectively in front of Elara, his body trembling with the effort to restrain the beast within him.

Kieran: (Snarling) You… you're the one behind this. The one who cursed me.

The figure nods, its eyes burning brighter with malice.

Figure: (Slyly) Yes. I have waited for centuries for this night. The full moon. The curse. You were always meant to be mine, Kieran. You were always meant to become what you fear the most—the monster within. And now… it is time.

Kieran's body shudders, the beast fighting against him, but Elara stands strong, her voice cutting through the tension like a beacon of hope.

Elara: (Stepping forward) You won't have him. You won't control him. We're not afraid of you. Whatever you are, whatever darkness you hold, we will fight back.

The figure chuckles darkly, a sound that chills Elara's bones, but she stands her ground.

Figure: (Mockingly) You think you can stop this? You think you can stop me? The beast is already in you, Kieran. The transformation is inevitable.

Kieran growls low in his throat, his body convulsing as the beast inside him claws to be released, but Elara doesn't step back. She grabs his hand tightly, refusing to let him go.

Elara: (Whispering) We will fight together. You are not alone, Kieran. We will defeat this. Together.

Kieran looks at her, his eyes wild, torn between the man he is and the beast he's afraid to become. But in her gaze, he sees the truth. There is no escaping this fate—not without her by his side. He lets out a final, anguished cry as the last of the moon slips below the horizon, and the world holds its breath for the coming storm.

www.ingramcontent.com/pod-product-compliance
Lightning Source LLC
LaVergne TN
LVHW021047100526
838202LV00079B/4750